To Anne Lee,
   Best wishes,
      Louise E. Gray

REFLECTIONS:
WINDOWS
ON THE PAST

REFLECTIONS:
WINDOWS
ON THE PAST

LOUISE EUBANK GRAY

Brunswick

Copyright© 1995 by Louise Eubank Gray

All rights reserved. No part of this book may be reproduced in any form or by any means, electronic or mechanical, including photocopying or by any informational storage or retrieval system, without written permission from the author and the publisher.

These articles and essays have previously appeared in *The Daily Press, The Fredericksburg Times,* and *Pleasant Living,* and are published with permission.

Photographs, except as otherwise noted, by Mary Steed Sutton Ewell.

Library of Congress Cataloging-in-Publication Data

Gray, Louise E.
    Reflections : windows on the past / Louise Eubank Gray.
       p.   cm.
    Includes bibliographical references (p.).
    ISBN 1-55618-146-9 (acid-free)
    1. Virginia—Social life and customs.   I. Title.
F231.G73   1994
975.5—dc20   94-38895
                                                  CIP

Published in the United States of America

by

Brunswick Publishing Corporation
1386 Lawrenceville Plank Road
Lawrenceville, Virginia 23868

*This book is dedicated to
relatives, neighbors, friends,
and future readers who
share a love of the past.*

"... Now twittering swallows seek their nests."

Day's End

The barn stands black in silhouette
against the sun's red afterglow.
One star hangs low in darkening sky.
Now twittering swallows seek their nests
of mud beneath low-hanging eaves
and pigeons find their raftered roosts.
The weary horse is munching hay
in straw-filled stall, his labor done.
Our cows chew cuds in quiet ease.
My cat sits motionless, alert
for stirrings of unwary mice.
A lantern hangs outside a stall
while practiced hand from udders full
draws tinkling stream of milk to pail.
I count the stars as one by one
they slowly prick the velvet dark.
I watch the fireflies' winking lights,
and listen for the milker's tread.
At last he comes with foaming pail,
the lantern casting pools of light.
I join my father joyously
and skip beside him to our door
where rest, and peace, and love await.
We gather for the evening meal
and with bowed heads we thank the Lord
for food and home and all things good.

Acknowledgments

First, I wish to thank the editors of *The Daily Press, Pleasant Living,* and *The Fredericksburg Times* for permission to use the articles and essays previously appearing in those publications. In particular, I am indebted to Joan Marble, news assistant, and to Kathy Van Mullekom, "Neighbors" editor of *The Daily Press,* for their assistance and cooperation.

I also wish to thank the many people who provided information from personal recollections and who shared their expertise on various subjects. Without their generous help this volume would not have been possible.

In addition, I wish to thank my typist, Roxanne Haden, for her cheerful and willing help in typing and retyping these manuscripts, and Mary Steed Sutton Ewell, whose interesting and appropriate photographs greatly enhance this book.

Contents

Day's End	vii
Introduction	1
I. DAILY LIVING	3
Open-Hearth Cooking	4
The Ice House	7
Butter-Making	9
Corning Herring	13
Before Automatic Washers	16
Without Indoor Plumbing	20
Needlework	23
The Hand-Held Fan	27
Sunday Dinner	30
Weather Terms	34
Feasting	37
II. WORK	41
Hand-Dug Wells	42
The Blacksmith	45
Grist Mills	48
The Versatile Apple	52
Making Sorghum Molasses	55
Whitewash, the Poor Man's Paint	58
Lumbering	61
Commerce*	66
III. CHURCH AND SCHOOL	69
Christ Episcopal Church, Mathews	70
An Early Baptist Church	73
Revivals	76
Public Education Moved Slowly in Virginia	79
Rappahannock Industrial Academy	83
Writing Instruments	87

IV. TRANSPORTATION / TRAVEL 91
    Sailing Vessels 92
    Ferries 96
    River Highways and Rolling Roads 98
    Ordinaries, Taverns and Inns 100
    Bridges Over the Dragon 103
    Steamboat Era 107
    Top Buggies and Surreys 111

V. LOCAL HISTORY 115
    Man of Mystery* 116
    The Colonial Militia 119
    The Discovery of Tobacco 121
    The Tobacco Trade 123
    King and Queen County, 1691-1991 126
    Ambush and Arson in King and Queen County 130
    Union Troops and the Dragon 140
    Fort Nonsense 143
    Court Days 146

VI. POTPOURRI 151
    To Love a Place** 152
    Feather Beds Were Luxuries** 157
    Two Virginia Botanists 162
    Church Bells 165
    Country Doctors** 169
    Jousting Is not Dead** 173

Bibliography 177

---

* These essays were first published in the *Fredericksburg Times*.

** These essays were orignally published in *Pleasant Living* magazine.

Introduction

The essays and articles in this collection, with several exceptions, first appeared in "Neighbors," Middle Peninsula Section, a feature of *The Daily Press*, published in Newport News, Virginia. Entitled "Reflections," the pieces began in March 1990 and are continuing at the present time. They have dealt with subjects of local history, education, religion, customs, and our local Virginia lifestyle. The style in the beginning was carefully objective, but it has frequently become subjective as the topics became more familiar to me personally.

All of the pieces are factual. My purpose has always been to provide a window on the past. Life is changing so rapidly that the present generation has no conception of what life was like at the beginning of this century. Regardless of its rigors, or perhaps because of them, this life style produced men and women of strong character who were independent, honest, industrious, and reliable. We should not lose sight of the conditions that molded such people. The collected essays will take you back in time and allow you to see how we coped without the benefits of modern technology in the home, in the work place, and in other associations.

My sources have been varied. Many articles required research into historical reference works. For instance, the colonial militia, the tobacco trade, sailing vessels, early bridges and ferries were carefully researched through local records and other sources. Many pieces included interviews with elderly people who were willing to share their personal experiences. Often they allowed me to quote them, and their comments added color and authenticity to the article. In addition I have been able to provide from my own experience, eye-witness accounts of tasks which were part of our daily living. My purpose has been to give the reader a glimpse of the past as I knew it.

Many people have helped me and I owe them a debt of gratitude for their willingness to share their experiences and memories, recognizing, as I do, that our former way of life seems incredible to our young friends and neighbors.

Response from the reading public has been rewarding. Friends and acquaintances mention their pleasure in having memories revived; new-comers to our area express appreciation because they have gained knowledge of how people in Tidewater Virginia lived before the marvels of modern technology.

I trust that the reading public will find information, enjoyment, and insight into a way of life that forms the foundation, the wisdom, and the greatness of the past and of our present society.

Louise Eubank Gray
Saluda, Virginia
November 15, 1994

Daily Living

Open-Hearth Cooking

A recent ice storm with the resulting loss of electrical power to much of eastern Virginia brought to many people a taste of pioneer life which was enlightening but inconvenient. Some households fared much better than others, but almost everyone had an experience to tell of how he coped without electricity.

Homes which had a fireplace and a stack of wood on hand were much better off than those with nothing but a kerosene heater, a camp stove or some other device. Many homes, however, were entirely dependent upon electricity for heat, light, and cooking; these people were actually in need of outside help.

How did our forefathers manage, we wonder? Perhaps the most primitive form of cooking used by the earliest colonists was on an open fire to bake ash-cake or hoe cake. Open hearth cooking came later.

The hoe-cake was a mixture of cornmeal, salt and water formed into a cake and baked on the blade of a hoe before an open fire. The ash cake was baked directly in the fire; however, a slightly more sophisticated product was wrapped in cabbage leaves before baking. This suggests a homestead with a vegetable patch and a fireplace. Corn pone is the modern version of the legendary ash cake.

Having read of ash cakes, I once asked my father, born in 1880, if he knew how to make one. It was a rainy Sunday afternoon, and my parents and I, a young girl, were enjoying an open fire in the living room. He agreed to humor me by baking an ash cake on the hearth though I doubt that he had had much experience. Perhaps he had heard of it from his father, who as a soldier in the Confederate Army, had been glad to get even an ash cake at times.

We went to the kitchen, mixed a cup of meal, some salt and enough water to make a cake that could be shaped in his hands. Back in the living room, he brushed the ashes away from a brick, laid the cake on it, flattened it a little, covered it with ashes and then live coals. After about ten minutes when we thought it was done, he brushed off the coals, put it on a plate and took it back to the kitchen where he speared it with a fork and ran cold water over it to wash off the loose ashes. Eager with curiosity and anticipation, I cut the gray, unappealing lump into quarters and tasted it. It was edible, but barely. Needless to say one ash cake demonstration was enough, but the experience increased my appreciation of the hardships of the early settlers.

Visit Colonial Williamsburg, Wakefield, the Washington home in Richmond County or Stratford, the Lee home, and you get a different picture. There you see a working kitchen complete with an enormous fireplace equipped with spit, crane, pothooks and trivets. The black iron cooking utensils, which many of us remember but have replaced with more attractive looking pieces, were suited to open hearth cooking. They were sturdy, did not warp, and held heat well. They came in numerous shapes for different purposes: the black iron spider, tea kettle, griddle, deep cooking pot with handle that could be suspended from a pot hook and so on. Such kitchens belonged to the wealthy, but others cooked with far less equipment.

Daniel Boone, and explorers like him, ate ash cake; Abraham Lincoln's parents had a log cabin with fireplace by which he read at night and did his sums on the back of a shovel using a charred coal. No doubt ash cake was common there too.

Open hearth cooking continued until the 19th century was well advanced. I have in my possession a brass kettle which belonged to my grandfather. It has an eleven and a half inch handle, a depth of five inches, and a diameter of eleven inches. Originally, it had three legs and a rounded bottom since it was not intended for use on a stove. My mother had the legs sawed off, to my sorrow, so that she could use it on her wood burning kitchen range although she had to remove the stove lid in order for it to sit level. She used it to make cucumber pickle because it produced a bright green color. I would not consider it safe today, but I never heard of anyone suffering ill-effects from eating her pickle.

She told me:

> Papa baked his pound cakes in this kettle. He would rake live coals out on the hearth to form a thin layer and place the pot filled with batter over them. As the coals cooled he would push them aside and add more embers. He turned the pot from time to time so that all sides received heat from the blazing fire. Baking a cake required constant attention, patience and plenty of know-how.

It seems amazing to me that a cake could be baked in this manner. I do not always produce a perfect cake even in a temperature controlled oven.

Our recent experience with fireplace cooking was short-lived. Anyone who had been a Boy Scout, Girl Scout, or camper was pressed into service to recall their cooking skills with real appreciation by the family. From it all, we gained new respect for the expertise of old-time cooks.

In addition, many came to realize how much they depended on the television for entertainment to the exclusion of family activities, such as, crafts, games, and conversation.

There was a positive side to this experience, however. The ice storm seemed to bring out the best in us. Neighbors showed real concern for each other, hauling wood and water, lending equipment, shopping for the elderly, entertaining friends who had no alternative source of heat and doing other helpful acts. Churches with heat opened their doors, schools became shelters and electricians and volunteers worked long hours in intense cold to restore electricity for our use. Thus the discomforts and inconveniences revealed the good side of human nature and brought us closer together in good will.

The Ice House

Lack of refrigeration was a serious problem for everyone from the days of the early settlers until the advent of manufactured ice. The first colonists found the heat and humidity of Virginia summers almost unbearable and were the first to attempt to carry winter ice over into summer. Archaeologists have found crude pits which they believe were used to store ice for use during at least part of the hot weather.

The Governor's Palace in Williamsburg (c. 1700) features an above-ground ice house, a small brick structure covered on three sides with earth to provide insulation. On the fourth side is a small door to give access to the contents.

The great Colonial plantations stored ice also, but they used the opposite approach. A deep pit was dug, often in the woods where shade was constant, ice was packed between layers of insulating materials and a low roof covered the contents. There was usually an ice pond nearby; it was made by damming a fresh water stream to flood a low-lying area. The water did not have to be deep. Ice was easier to harvest from a shallow pond.

The ice house I remember was built on the pattern of one in use in my grandfather's day. The new one was constructed to serve two families: ours and my uncle's and it was located for the convenience of both households.

The pit was about thirty feet deep with a six-foot well in the center for drainage. It was lined on all four sides with logs placed vertically from the bottom to ground level. The sides sloped outward so that it was wider at the top. The bottom, as I recall, was covered with a floor of logs laid side by side and a second layer laid in the opposite direction. This kept them in place and allowed water from the melting ice to drain into the center well. On this floor were piled several feet of wheat straw, pine needles or sawdust. The ice pit was covered with a low slab roof; a door in the A-roof opened to the dark interior.

Ice was harvested in winter when a period of prolonged cold produced ice three or more inches thick. The ice was cut in huge blocks, loaded on a wagon and hauled to the ice house, where it was placed between layers of straw. Sometimes it took several freezes to fill the ice house. The object was to have enough ice for cooling drinks and freezing ice cream to last all summer.

In hot weather as meal time approached I would be sent to the ice house to get ice for dinner. I had to dig through the thick straw with a pitchfork, find a block of ice, chip off some pieces and run home with them before they melted. The ice was covered with bits of straw and had to be washed off, and chipped into small pieces to be used at the table. Speed was important because there was no way to keep it from melting.

As the season advanced, the level in the ice house fell so that by late summer it was necessary to descend a ladder to reach the ice. One day after getting my bucket filled, I saw a huge black snake between me and the ladder. Trapped, I cowered in the corner afraid to take my eyes off the snake which kept its beady eyes fixed on me and occasionally ran out its forked tongue.

After what seemed an interminable wait, my father came to my rescue and we carried the ice to the house to the waiting dinner guests.

One of our summer delights was homemade ice cream made possible by the supply of ice in the ice house.

Mother made a rich custard of eggs, milk, cream, and sugar and added fresh peaches in season. This was put into a two-gallon metal cylinder which fitted into a wooden bucket which held crushed ice. A crank turned the cylinder in an icy brine. This required man power but it was not hard to find willing workers who looked forward to the treat at the end of the activity.

Modern refrigeration is one of the most important technological advances of the 20th century, but the passing of the ice house closed a colorful chapter in rural life.

Butter-Making

Butter making has become a lost art for most modern women, but it was only one among many homemaking skills which their grandmothers possessed. Homemade or "country butter" is a rarity today. Even owners of dairy farms market the whole milk and buy butter for family use.

Rural children have become so accustomed to buying milk and milk products from the supermarket that some do not even associate cows with their products. I once asked a group of kindergartners what, to me, was a simple, almost silly, question: Where does butter come from? The children's first answer was unanimous: "From the store." Questioned further, one responded "from trees," but no one thought of milk or cows.

Two generations ago the answers would have been correct because most children would have seen mother or grandmother make butter. They would have known what buttermilk was as well as clabber and some would have known how to milk a cow or care for milk products. How times have changed!

Most farmers in the early decades of this century kept a cow or two to insure a constant supply of milk for the household and possibly to sell small amounts of surplus to a neighbor. Fresh milk might bring ten cents a quart, clabber ten cents a gallon, and butter twenty or twenty-five cents a pound. When men were paid $1.00 for a day's work, anything that supplemented the income was welcome.

When a calf was born, the cow was said to have "come fresh." For the first week the nursing calf got the milk; afterwards the cow was milked night and morning providing milk for both calf and owner.

The fresh milk was poured into large pans or bowls and left overnight for the cream to rise. (Cream separators came later.) Next day the cream was skimmed off, and the "skim milk" was fed to the hogs. When enough cream, slightly soured, had accumulated, it was time for churning.

Churns varied in design from large wooden ones to some as simple as a gallon glass jar in which the cream was shaken back and forth until the butter formed. The type most common for home use in my neighborhood was a two or three gallon stoneware jar with a handmade wooden lid that fitted the jar securely. The dasher, also handmade, was a flat wooden circle with several holes evenly spaced around it; a handle about thirty inches long was fixed in the center. The handle passed through a hole in the top. A commercial type, introduced somewhat later as an improvement, was a large glass container with paddles inside turned by a crank on the lid.

Churning meant sitting by the churn and working the dasher up and down with a rhythmical stroke until the fat globules in the cream began to collect into flecks of butter and finally into a thick mass. Sometimes it took an hour, sometimes less, for the butter "to come."

The buttermilk would then be poured into a pitcher for drinking or making biscuits or cornbread. The butter would be turned into a bowl to be washed several times with cold water to remove all the milk. A handmade cedar butter paddle was used to work the butter into a cohesive mass. This was an important step because if the milk was not removed, the butter would soon have a strong taste and eventually turn rancid. Next, it was lightly salted. Salt not only flavored the butter but drew out traces of milk. It was set aside until next day when it was worked again before being pressed into one pound or half-pound molds to shape it. Turned out on a plate, the print might carry a daisy or a sheaf or wheat, a decoration from the mold.

Some careful housewives worked the butter again on the third day. By this time the salt would have drawn off more liquid, and the butter would be firm and solid. It would keep longer with no change in flavor. Housewives who sold surplus butter took the time to produce a high quality product which would enhance their reputation for good butter.

Frances Moore Anderton of Saluda has in her possession a record book kept by her father, Frank Moore, in which he noted the sale of various farm products. An entry in 1914 showed butter sold for twenty-five cents a pound. In 1918 it was forty cents a pound, the result of rising prices during World War I. Eventually it went to fifty cents but declined during the Depression.

Butter-making Tools. From left, churn with handmade wooden lid and dasher, butter bowl, buttermilk pitcher, handmade cedar paddle and one half pound butter mold and printer.

Making butter in summer, before refrigeration, was different. Butter has a low melting point, and in hot weather becomes soft and hard to work. Ice from the ice house might be used in the washing steps to harden it, but it was impossible to mold it to keep its shape. Well-to-do households resorted to two-part butter dishes often seen in antique shops today. The lower part held ice and the upper part a pat of butter, but this was only a mealtime solution. Some people used a cooler or tin with a close fitting top, filled it with butter and hung it by a rope in the well. The same thing was often done with cream to keep it from souring too rapidly before churning.

In winter the problems were reversed. Churning might not take as long, washing and working the butter might be easier, but on the second and third days it required real physical strength to work it. Kept in a cold place, the butter would at first be as hard and unyielding as a rock. After it was put in the printer, it could be unmolded, wrapped in butter paper, and easily handled.

Making and caring for butter taxed the skills of housewives for centuries. Some sought the spring and set the churn there to cool it before churning, some made use of a cellar if they had one, some were fortunate enough to have specially constructed dairies, but the problems were always great. The marvels of refrigeration have made life easier for most people and have certainly resulted in better butter.

Corning Herring

In March and April herring come into the Chesapeake Bay tributaries in large numbers to spawn. For centuries they have made this seasonal run into local rivers. The Rappahannock, the Pamunkey, the Mattaponi and the Chicahominy Rivers swarm with them.

The Indians relied upon them for food and so did the first Virginia settlers. They learned to salt them to have a supply for winter also. The colonists' survival depended upon preserving enough food in various ways for winter use. Drying and salting food soon became a way of life.

By this time of year fifty or sixty years ago most rural families were busy curing fish, following a tradition of their ancestors. Without modern refrigeration and supermarkets, feeding a family a varied and healthful diet required canning, drying, preserving and salting a variety of foods. A staple item of diet was salt fish, convenient and cheap. Herring could be bought then for a cent a piece; today they cost at least five times that amount.

The curing process was relatively simple, but there were variations in the methods and recipes in use.

Today Jeff Jones, a resident of Tunstall in New Kent County, uses a method modified to modern needs. When the fish begin to run he and George Bowman put their nets into the Pamunkey River.

"The weather controls when the run begins," said Jones. "We put out shad and herring nets and catch right many—not like it used to be, of course, but we're not fishing to sell. We do it for fun and to get fish for the club and for ourselves."

Jones and Bowman belong to the Waterloo Hunt Club made up of local men. The club owns a building near Tunstall; their clubhouse is named for the old Waterloo house nearby. A favorite breakfast of the members, enjoyed before a hunt is salt herring and hush puppies, traditional winter fare. Jones and his friend catch the fish and cure them for the club.

"We scale the fish and filet them—cut a two-inch strip down each side—that way the pieces have almost no bones," he said. "We give the rest of the fish to the dogs. Then we salt them down in plastic buckets."

"They have to be soaked overnight and the water changed several times to get rid of the salt before cooking," Jones continued. "We roll them in Martha White corn meal and deep fry them. Nice and brown and crisp, they can't be beat."

Asked about the roe, Jones answered, "We can it or freeze it."

Betsy James Simmons of Saluda follows a recipe in use before the Civil War and probably even before that. It came from her great-grandfather, E. T. Purkins, who lived at "Plainview," a 300 acre estate just outside Saluda. His recipe is as follows:

   200 herring
   1 qt. black molasses (King Po-To-Ric)
   1/2 lb. black pepper
   2 oz. red pepper
   2 oz. saltpeter
   2 lbs. dark brown sugar

Mix all these ingredients and warm on the stove. Scale the fish, remove head and tail and drain (remove entrails). Put them in a tub of salt water that will bear an egg (when the brine will float a hen egg, it will keep anything), and soak overnight. Drain on a board and pack in containers. Put a layer of salt at the bottom, a layer of fish, another layer of salt, then pour the prepared mixture over the layers. Continue until all fish have been used.

"Grandpa's recipe has gone far and wide," said Bettie Woodward James, Mrs. Simmons's mother. "People who grew up on salt fish never lose the taste for it. Some love it enough to cure a few for their own use even today. It's a form of nostalgia. You never get over your raising, I guess," she ended, laughing.

Stoneware jars were the containers preferred by our grandparents because they were unaffected by the salt. Discarded plastic buckets make ideal containers today.

The Purkins' recipe left the fish whole with the roe inside. They were soaked overnight in a large quantity of water, drained, dried, dipped in corn meal or flour and fried in a black iron spider (frying pan) in his day. Following tradition, Mrs. James uses a spider, but some modern housewives maintain that an electric fry pan will do a satisfactory job.

Marie Major Anton of Saluda said the method used by her mother, Mrs. John Major, was slightly different from both of these already described.

"She cleaned the fish, then opened them, split them by the backbone so they would lie flat, and packed them between layers of salt in a crock," she said.

This resembled the method I remember. My mother followed practices long in use in our family. She salted the roe separately, however. To prepare it for the table she boiled the roe in water to remove some salt, poured off the water, added bacon fat to the spider, mashed the roe, added eggs and scrambled it. Thus diluted the mixture was not too salty. Served with bacon and batter-bread, it was a breakfast special.

The need for preserving food in this way has diminished, but habits die hard, and many people long for old-fashioned salt fish and put up a few by the recipe each fondly remembers.

Before Automatic Washers

The automatic washing machine and drier now have taken the drudgery from doing the family laundry, but things were very different before the advent of modern technology. There were good reasons for the Saturday night bath and weekly change of clothing then for doing the washing was an arduous task not to be undertaken more than once a week.

It is true that washing machines were available, but they were cumbersome and not in wide use. Ruth Bowden St. John recalls that her father bought one for his wife about 1915:

> It was hand-powered and stood on four legs. The wooden tub was round and about the size of a regular wash tub. The paddles inside were wood too, and there was a wheel on the outside which you had to turn to rotate the paddles. Aunt Marthy Reed, who came every week to do the laundry, thought it was the finest thing she'd ever seen. It did save scrubbing clothes on the wash board, but you had to draw off the water and refill the tub to rinse and to blue. The wringer had to be operated by hand too.

John M. Moore of Stormont says he has a similar model stored in his barn.

Washing machines have gone through many improvements to reach the almost labor-free designs in use today.

Even though these machines saved some labor many people continued to use methods in use for centuries.

In most households Monday was washday. The soiled clothes replaced after the Saturday night bath with clean ones for the coming week were gathered up early along with household laundry for the weekly wash. Most homes did not have indoor plumbing so first, the laundress had to draw several buckets of water from the well to heat for the process. Some families had a wash-house, a small separate building in the yard, equipped with a stove, where the laundry was done; in fine weather some preferred to heat the water in a big iron pot over a fire and do the whole job outside. Some families sent the laundry out to be done by a laundress in the neighborhood who "took in washing." She washed and ironed the clothes during the week and returned them on Friday or Saturday. This arrangement freed the housewife from two days devoted to this laborious process but it had its drawbacks. If none of these arrangements existed, the whole operation might have had to take place in the kitchen, space on the cookstove being shared possibly by a pot of beans simmering for dinner and the lard tin heating wash water. No matter where the washing was done two or three large washtubs were needed. The first contained a corrugated washboard on which the clothes were scrubbed to remove heavily soiled spots, the second held rinse water to remove soap and dirty water from the first washing, and the third contained bluing water to improve whiteness.

The laundress started with the white clothes, usually less soiled and requiring less scrubbing. These were washed, wrung by hand, and transferred to the rinse water. More heavily soiled work clothes were soaped and placed in the first tub to soak while she took the first lot through the rinsing and bluing processes. If the family was large, there might be more than one tub of each. Often the laundress felt the need to boil some of the pieces. These were placed in the lard tin or boiler with soap or even a weak solution of lye and boiled to remove stains or dinginess, the result of a residue of soap and hard water left from previous laundering. Boiling produced a very white, sparkling line of clothes, a matter of pride for the housewife. Extreme care had to be used in boiling, however; the clothes were stirred with a stick kept for the purpose and also used to lift them from the boiling water into the rinse water. The amount of lye had to be carefully gauged too or the clothes would be damaged.

The washing process was slow involving drawing quantities of water, emptying heavy tubs, and handling each item of clothing by hand. The final stage was starching. Many pieces were put through a starch water to give them extra body, and make them resist soil.

The clean clothes were then hung on the clothesline to dry. Wind and sun, which whitened the clothes, hastened the drying and gave the laundry an added freshness and pleasant odor.

In many cases the housewife had made the soap which she used. She saved grease from bacon, ham trimmings, chicken fat or beef tallow. She dissolved a can of Red Devil lye in about three quarts of water and then added the grease. The proper proportion of lye and fat was very important; if too much lye was used the soap would be strong, hard on the hands, and damaging to the articles laundered in it. The action of the lye dissolved the grease. It was brought to a boil and gradually it thickened. When the mixture was thick enough, it was set aside to cool a little, then poured into shallowpans, and left to harden. Later it was cut into blocks and set away for use during the next several months.

Starch was usually made at home too. Commercial starches were also available but it was more economical for a thrifty housewife to make her own. She mixed flour and water to form a thin paste, poured it into a kettle of hot water, and boiled it until it thickened. The mixture was strained to remove lumps and thinned to a consistency proper for different purposes. For instance, a thin starch was used for pillowcases, petticoats and table linens.

By the end of the day a mountain of laundry would have been washed, boiled, rinsed, blued, starched, hung on the line, dried, and taken in. That evening the housewife would spend some time replacing buttons, sewing up rips, patching or darning in preparation for the next day's work: ironing.

Fortunate was the woman who had help with this exhausting task, but many women undertook it weekly, washing for households ranging in size from three or four to a dozen. No wonder the children were admonished to "keep your clothes clean," and changes usually occurred weekly.

Wash tub and scrub board.

Without Indoor Plumbing

Electricity was in use in cities long before the conveniences it made possible reached many rural areas. Keeping a home supplied with water in the days before indoor plumbing was for centuries a sizable job. The well was located fairly close to the house, but the water had to be carried by the bucket into the house. Early wells had a pulley suspended from a frame above the opening and water was drawn by lowering the bucket into the well and pulling it up. Later, a pump operated by hand constituted a tremendous labor saver, but either way, water had to be taken indoors by man-power.

The kitchen required the largest amount of water; it was necessary for cleaning and preparing food, cooking, drinking, dish washing and other needs. On wash days it was often the center of this activity.

Water had to be carried to all the bedrooms, usually a chore for one of the children. Each room had a washstand with the following standard equipment: a large pitcher and washbowl, a smaller pitcher for drinking water, a mug to hold toothbrushes, a soap dish and a large slop jar for waste water. This had to be carried out and emptied daily. The washstand sets were often colorful and attractive and are much in demand today by antique hunters.

The washstand sometimes had a towel bar attached or a free standing towel-rack to hold washcloths and towels for daily partial baths.

The Saturday night bath was a reality and not a joke as it sometimes sounds today. A complete bath required much more water to be carried upstairs and brought down again, adding to the not inconsiderable labor involved.

Bedrooms often had two to four occupants; bathing was done by turn and in installments: first the upper part of the body, next the lower part and feet last. Modesty required that the bather never be completely uncovered. The whole bath for each person probably required no more than a gallon of water, but the total was sizable in terms of supply and disposal. Shampooing the hair was usually done in the kitchen for convenience to the water supply and for disposal. (Thrown out back door!)

Laundry was done outside in good weather. Big tubs were filled from the well and water was heated over an open fire. Washing clothes indoors required more work to bring in water, heat it on the cook stove, wash the clothes through several waters, and dispose of the waste. On washdays the kitchen would be given over to the laundry, excluding all but the simplest cooking.

Lack of indoor plumbing also demanded the use of small outhouses located in an inconspicuous place. In use for centuries, strangely enough, these outbuildings are seldom mentioned in the literature of the past. However, in the writings of William Byrd of Westover references do appear to the "Necessary house." Although these were an essential part of the great plantations of Colonial days, historians have failed to include them when describing the dependencies of the manor houses, such as the smoke house, the dairy, or the wash house. Architecturally unimportant, they were, nevertheless, an integral part of the lifestyle of both rich and poor before modern times.

Known by a variety of names, some crude, some humorous, some euphemistic, outdoor privies were a part of every family's living arrangements in rural areas before electricity reached them. Many of us who grew up in this era remember them vividly if not fondly. One that I was familiar with was called "the garden house," an apt name because it was located in the garden. To reach it one opened the gate, followed the picket fence to the far corner where the outhouse stood, obscured by a clump of box bushes. The walk to this destination, if leisurely, was pleasant. Gooseberries bordered the path and one could pick a few in season. In spring a row of strawberries offered tempting fruit for the taking. Inclement weather made the trip down the garden path less enjoyable, but some things could not be governed by weather.

The building itself was commodious and satisfactory. It had a comfortable, well-worn seat with three holes in graduated sizes: small, medium and large. It provided reading matter of sorts, not current always, but educational or entertaining. Standard equipment were a box of lime and an outdated Sears, Roebuck catalogue. Its thin pages when rumpled and rubbed vigorously became a soft, satisfactory paper.

During the make-work projects of FDR's New Deal in the 1930s, building these outhouses provided work for some unemployed people who were paid to erect them free of cost for families without such facilities. The standard size had a crescent moon on the door for light and decoration. Cartoonists soon made use of this design as a stock figure to represent primitive living conditions.

Some homeowners, unused to such refinements, were reluctant recipients of the new additions. One old fellow viewed his completed building with displeasure. "Now," he said, "I'd like to see you make me use it."

Although such conditions seem far in the past, unfortunately there are families living today who still depend upon the "necessary houses" or privies as did our ancestors.

The Northern Neck-Middle Peninsula Area Agency on Aging, a non-profit organization assisting the elderly, has a program for upgrading or installing indoor plumbing for area citizens. Wayne Talley, in charge of the project, states that within the last four years the agency has rehabilitated 190 area homes. "There are ninety households now on the waiting list," Talley says.

In a growing population, environmental needs of sanitation and good health require that William Byrd's "necessary house" ceases to be necessary.

Needlework

Women have always occupied themselves with needlework. Every culture has produced distinctive creations characteristic of a period, a region or a life style. In the 17th century in America the focus was on the practical needs of the home; fancy work came later.

Quilting, an early form of needlework, was born of necessity in colonial times. Trade restrictions by England forbade the importation of textiles from any other source; likewise looms for home weaving could not he imported legally. Textile materials were, therefore, scarce. Nothing was thrown away. The old saying: "Eat it up, wear it out, make it do" was put into practice in all but the most affluent households. Clothing was passed down, clothes were cut down for younger children and even the scraps were saved. Every home had a scrap-bag where pieces of cloth were saved for quilt pieces or rugs.

The crazy quilt was probably the first type produced from the scrap-bag. It followed no pattern; pieces were sewed together until a bed-sized cover resulted; this was the quilt top. The finished quilt consisted of three layers: top, filling and lining.

Quilting was done on a rectangular wooden frame held together at the corners with clamps. The lining was placed on the quilting frame first and stitched around the frame to hold it in place, next the cotton filling was put on the lining and basted into place; then the top was basted on. The three layers were stitched together to keep them taut before the actual quilting began.

The earliest quilts intended for warmth instead of a display of fine needlework did not make use of a variety of quilting stitches as did later ones. The need to finish the cover quickly led to the quilting bees where neighbors came to help with the work. They served a social purpose also by bringing women together for a day of conversation, a good meal, and a cooperative job to do.

By the early 19th century quilt-making had become an artistic and creative outlet for the makers. Elaborate patterns and fine stitches characterized the quilts which were used as coverlets for decoration more often than for warmth. Patterns varied from simple ones such as the nine-patch and the pinwheel to more difficult ones with intriguing names: drunkard's path, flying geese, grandmother's flower garden, and the dragon fly. Others were more descriptive: wedding ring, basket, or log cabin.

The quality of a fine quilt is measured today by the number of quilting stitches per inch. A wide variety of quilting stitches may be employed. One book listed twenty-six different stitches which might be recognized on 19th century quilts. By then it had become an art form. Quilts of this period have become highly prized collector's items. The progression of skill from those needed to construct a quilt for warmth in the 1600s to those required to produce an artistic product of heirloom quality was slow but steady.

Rugs were also made during the period when textiles were scarce and money even scarcer. Housewives taxed their ingenuity to make articles to enhance their homes when all they had to offer were labor and time. Handmade rugs were of several types but hooked and braided were the most popular.

The hooked rug was made by pulling narrow strips of woolen cloth through a cloth foundation, usually burlap, with a special needle. Patterns could be drawn on the foundation cloth to create designs, but the braided rugs were more durable but without a set design.

I am more familiar with the braided rug because I had an aunt who was especially good at making them. I have seen her cutting up her husband's worn-out woolen pants and coats and woolen skirts and jackets of the ladies of the family into strips about an inch wide. These were sewed together to form long pieces. She folded the strip so that the raw edges came together, then folded the piece again and wound them tightly into a ball. When she had three balls of similar size, she braided them together as one plaited hair. When she had a large ball she started in the center coiling the plaited strips to form a circle or an oval and stitching them together with strong thread. Great care had to be taken at this point to keep the tension even so that the piece would lie flat on the floor. The colors formed a random pattern although sometimes bands of the same color might be achieved. Such rugs were reversible and lasted for years. The homey effect of such rugs appears in commercial braided rugs available today.

By the 1900s the need to make rugs and quilts to meet practical needs diminished but the pleasure of doing fine handwork continued. Women prided themselves on their abilities with the needle. One author wrote, "the mark of a well trained young woman was recognized by the fine stitching and elaborate diagrams of her sampler."

Samplers were a popular form of needlework on which the maker displayed a sample of the embroidery stitches which she could do. They were usually made on a piece of hand woven linen which varied in size according to the skill of the lady. A sampler displaying fourteen different stitches was not unusual.

The pictorial sampler might show a building, people, birds, flowers and animals. A few were genealogical records but the alphabet sampler was the most common.

I have one made by my great-aunt dated 1828 and signed with her name. It measures 8½ by 13½ inches, is on handwoven natural linen using yellow and green thread. It has a row of capital letters, a row of figures up to ten, and a row of small letters. An elaborate border surrounds it. It does not display more than five or six different stitches according to my unskilled count, but I have prized it enough to have it framed.

Today quilting is extremely popular and beautiful, colorful patterns are available made by skilled needewomen. The

Amish are particularly noted for the beauty and workmanship of their quilts which sell for hundreds of dollars. The friendship quilt with each patch bearing the signature of the maker is a much-prized type. But collectors seek the handmade quilts of the 18th and 19th centuries which are the most valuable.

The Hand-Held Fan

Air conditioning has brought comfort to millions of people; in the comparatively short time since it was introduced it has become standard equipment in public buildings and many private homes. In fact, so spoiled have we become that some people refuse to attend public gatherings if the building is not air-conditioned.

Have we forgotten the days before AC when we resorted to all sorts of methods to keep cool? Though we have gained comfort, in the process, we have given up some once familiar things—notably fans.

Porch sitting has almost disappeared now, but there was a time when a shady screened porch where one might catch a stray breeze was a favorite spot on a hot day. We might shell beans there in the morning, entertain friends in the afternoon with cool drinks, fans, and conversation, swing lazily in the porch swing and watch the moon rise in the evening or even sleep there in periods of extreme heat at night. Unscreened porches were not much use after dark when mosquitoes came out in droves. Their constant buzzing sounded like a motor running and their vicious bites raised itching bumps. The screened porch was the epitome of comfort then.

But the simplest cooling device, the least expensive, the most convenient, and the easiest to use was the hand-held fan. Older people may remember that the fan was so common that it attracted no attention. A hostess kept a number on hand for guests, passing them around almost as soon as greetings were over. The church hymnal racks held a supply, and merchants provided them to their customers gratis. Of course, I am referring to the light-weight cardboard fan with the popsicle style handle. One side carried a colorful picture and the other advertising. Funeral homes seemed to have a monopoly on supplying church needs, confident that the message would be read as the fan was used.

There were other fans, however, more attractive in appearance and more personal. Almost every lady possessed a folding fan, which she carried in her handbag when she went to church, to pay calls or even to shop. Colorful, neat, and convenient, they were often cherished gifts that were passed down as heirlooms. Such fans were available in great variety and some filled special needs. For instance, the widow in mourning possessed a black one, and the bride might have a fancy white lace one as part of her trousseau; and little girls often had a child-sized fan. Mine was ivory, laced with blue ribbon and bore a delicate spray of blue flowers.

Fans held an important place in courtship. The popular young lady knew how to use hers with telling effect. It was a great prop. She might blush prettily behind her open fan upon receiving a compliment, or peep coyly around it, or smile flirtatiously over it.

It served another purpose sometimes too. The lady could toy with it endlessly to cover nervousness, drop it as a diversion or tap the gentleman playfully with it, unopened.

My mother used her closed fan to tap me gently on the head when I grew restless in church or less gently when I whispered.

Gentlemen used the palm leaf fan, a masculine accessory which stirred up a good breeze. Seated in church beside his lady love, her beau fanned her solicitously inquiring if she was "feeling any breeze."

Historically fans go back a long ways. Cleopatra in her barge on the Nile had her attendants stationed with palm leaves to fan her and Eastern monarchs required the same attention.

The folding fan may have originated in Japan and been introduced to this country by some enterprising ship captain who brought home gifts for his family.

The 1897 Sears, Roebuck Catalogue offered an assortment of fans—all made in Japan. Prices covered a wide range: a paper fan at three cents was described in the words of the catalogue as "12 inches long, beautifully decorated, strong split bamboo stick outside, handsomely corded." Other fans were made of parchment paper, silk, or feathers. One described as cocque feathers sold for forty-four cents, but the most elegant was "a genuine ostrich feather fan that will always look nice and curly" at $1.75. Some lady must have felt most handsomely attired for evening carrying such an unusual accessory.

It is a safe assumption that many of the fans treasured by the present generation as keepsakes were of Japanese origin and reached us by way of the Sears, Roebuck Catalogue which went into almost every home.

Other methods of keeping cool were used such as closing the windows, drawing the shades and closing the shutters, and were followed carefully by housewives in hot weather. The rooms achieved a cool dimness with sunlight and heat kept outside to a degree; after sundown the windows would be opened to let in cool air and closed again next morning, but nothing was as universally used as the hand-held fan.

Sunday Dinner

Do you remember Sunday dinner? It was usually the best meal of the week except for special occasions such as birthdays, anniversaries, and holidays and quite often included company: relatives, friends, and frequently the preacher.

I'm sure there are families which still enjoy the custom, but it lacks the universal quality it once had. Visit the local restaurants on Sunday and notice that they begin to fill soon after the morning church services end. Whole families come in to enjoy a meal together, freeing the homemaker from the preparation, serving, and cleaning up after a big meal.

There was a time, however, when the Sunday midday meal served at home was a firmly established custom, almost a ritual. It served more than one purpose; not only did it mean a leisurely social meal with time for conversation, but it was also a training period for the children in table manners and polite behavior.

Sunday dinner was served in the dining room on a table covered with a white linen table cloth and set with the best china and silver. The housewife prided herself on "setting a good table" by which she meant providing an abundance of good food. She was always prepared for unexpected guests on Sunday and often had that pleasure.

I recall that on one summer Sunday my mother fed twenty-two. A carload of relatives drove down from Richmond, arriving unannounced but beaming in anticipation of a warm reception. On this occasion we were hard pressed and resorted to opening a quart of sausage canned the previous winter because we were afraid the chicken wouldn't go around.

Those were the days before telephones were common and visitors phoned ahead to announce their coming. In addition, there were no convenience stores, or delis and the nearest restaurant was thirty miles away. For the housewife preparedness was essential.

In my childhood we drove six miles to church in our surrey. The trip took approximately an hour each way, so Sunday dinner was not served until afternoon. In hot weather all food had to be prepared that morning. Chickens had to be killed, picked, dressed and fried, and fresh vegetables, abundant then, had to be prepared. Mother usually baked a big batch of rolls and a cake on Saturday because these would not spoil overnight.

In cold weather things were a little easier; food could be baked the day before, but a favorite dessert, grated sweet potato pudding was always done on Sunday morning. My father grated the potatoes, dropping a cupful at a time into a pan of milk to keep the raw potatoes from turning dark. To this mother added sugar, eggs, flavoring and a generous amount of butter. It was cooked in a slow oven and might even be warm for dinner.

Often we would invite another family to come home from church to enjoy Sunday dinner with us. If there were too many to be seated at once, the children waited for the second table. However, they were often at the table with the adults who all subscribed to the adage: "Children should be seen and not heard." They listened to the conversation but were not allowed to enter in. In fact, their plates were filled and then they were ignored.

A friend, now in his 80s, recounts an incident when he, aged four, was seated far down the table from his accustomed seat by his mother; quietly he asked, "Please pass the biscuits." Ignored, he tried again and again until in desperation he stood on his chair and shouted, "If you've got any common sense, pass the biscuits." Horrified, his mother sent him from the table weeping loudly.

There was a positive side to this practice though. By listening, children learned about community affairs, religion, education, politics, traditions, and even gossip. They were recognized as part of the group eventually to become grown-ups with a place in the community. It is true that some topics were deemed not for the ears of children and conversation was carefully screened.

Children had been trained to sit quietly at the table, left hand in the lap, to eat daintily, to cross the knife and fork correctly on the plate and to ask to be excused when ready to leave the table. They had also been instructed in what was suitable table conversation and etiquette.

On summer afternoons visiting men left the dinner table to walk about the farm, look at the crops, visit the barn to see the new calf, or at a later date to inspect the new Ford car in the garage. The women washed the dishes, exchanged recipes, admired the garden, and talked. Having spent most of the previous week at home, they were ready for some adult conversation. Children occupied themselves in various ways. Games were frowned upon by some adults as unsuitable for Sunday activities; others were more lenient.

The custom of a special family meal on Sunday is well-established in our society. All Christian countries recognized the six-day work-week based on the Biblical commandment. "Six days shalt thou labor." In England, from which we have drawn most of our long-held customs, young people left home to take jobs "in service," returning on Sunday to visit. Church attendance was mandatory, and it was natural to assemble after church for a good meal together. The custom unified the family and strengthened family ties.

The failure of the entire family to gather at the table for a meal together is a serious loss to modern family life. Teenagers have so many activities scheduled after school or early evening that they are constantly coming and going. Even pre-teens are involved in Boy or Girl Scouts, ballet classes, music lessons, soccer, Little League or some other sport which require the parents to be either dropping them off or picking them up so that meals are seldom eaten together. Even weekends are used for a variety of activities which separate rather than unite families.

Perhaps all of these things are worthwhile, but we lose something in the doing. I think the custom of Sunday family dinners should be re-established and everyone required to be there dressed in "Sunday clothes" and exhibiting Sunday manners. Whether the meal is served at home or in a restaurant, all family members will benefit from the relaxed atmosphere and the togetherness of the occasion. As a result we might find that family relationships improve and our digestion as well.

Weather Terms

Blackberry winter my mother called it—those cold, damp, dreary days in May when blackberries bloom. The expression had a dichotomy of sorts; berry blossoms suggest spring rather than winter, but it is really vividly descriptive. A tangle of blackberry vines in full bloom resembles a snow bank; each blossom, turned to the pale sun, presents its circle of white petals, delicate, pure and snowy. The clouds hang low, the wind is chilly enough to cause one to draw his wraps more closely around him, and the dampness soaks into the very bones. Blackberry winter, in the days before central heat, brought the family to the kitchen to cluster around the wood-burning cook stove for its pleasant warmth. Farmers waited for it to pass before setting out tender tomato plants, and old heads wondered if there would be frost. "The spring of '98 was the worst; I remember the potatoes were all nipped by frost," said the grandfather nodding his head sagely because only he knew that once there actually was frost in May.

Blackberry winter appeared to last interminably, but it only seemed long because we eagerly waited for the warm days when spring smiled more brightly. Then the old goose brought her brood of yellow goslings to nip the tender grass. She stood majestically near the young ones giving instructions to choose only the tenderest blades of grass and leave the shoots of redroot or night shade. Blackberry winter ended as suddenly as it had begun and everyone rejoiced.

Weather terms are intriguing because of their aptness. Some observant persons, long gone, coined them and because of their unique appeal they lasted.

Mackerel sky is a good example of a term drawn from nature. What does a mackerel sky look like? When a gray, overcast sky has small breaks in the cloud-cover overlapping like the scales of a fish, you can be sure that rain is in the making—maybe a day off, but coming. Then the sky looks a little like the gray mackerel with its tight overlapping scales so it is really descriptive.

Mare's tails are the wispy clouds swept by the wind, a sign of clearing weather.

Every year we are entertained with speculations about the ground hog due to end his winter's sleep on February 2nd. According to an old tradition, if the day is sunny and he sees his shadow, he supposedly returns to his hole for six more weeks of winter. Nobody takes it too seriously but it is fun.

Groundhog's Day is a typical Americanism, but Dog Days is a much older expression. The ancients believed that the conjunction of the rising of the Dog Star, Sirius, and the sun caused the hot, humid days of July and August. Dogs were especially liable to go mad during Dog Days.

St. Swithin's Day, observed in England on July 15, provided another weather omen. It was a belief among the English peasantry that if it rained on St. Swithin's Day it would continue to rain for forty days.

"All signs fail in dry weather" was a familiar saying coined perhaps when predictions and signs did not come true.

Everyone remembers the rhyme:

> Red sky in the morning, sailors take warning.
> Thunder at night, sailors delight.

Perhaps this forecast came true as often as it failed, "Shirtsleeve weather," "two-coat morning," "hog-killing weather," may also be familiar to some. My mother often referred to "pneumonia weather," those deceptively warm days that occurred in winter occasionally. Then less cautions people would venture out without wraps, bare-headed, and catch a dreadful cold, maybe even pneumonia.

A crescent moon in a vertical position was called a wet moon. (The water would pour out of it.) A dry moon was one that was horizontal. Both terms are visually suggestive.

Indian summer, another Americanism, is generally beloved in all parts of the country. It describes those mild, warm, hazy days that come after the first frost when winter seems far away. It beckons us to go on a picnic, a hike, a sight-seeing drive or just a lazy day spent outdoors. Indian summer is a last gift before winter sets in.

Weather talk is still an absorbing topic, but we get our information from the newspaper, the radio, the television, or the cable weather channel. No doubt this is more scientific and often more accurate but is it as much fun? We have become passive receivers, unobservant, uninvolved—not even looking at the sky or feeling the wind. Old weather sayings have become interesting as folklore, like some tool found in a flea market, out-moded, useless, but entertaining as a conversation piece.

Some of us, however, still like to get our information firsthand. I enjoy a Maine weather stick, a rustic weather predictor from the backwoods of Maine purported to have been used by the Abanaki Indians. It appears to be a small branch from a tree, the species a carefully kept secret. It hangs on an outside wall exposed to the weather and bends down to foretell foul weather and points up for fair (unless you hang it upside down). Strangely enough, it is a very accurate predictor and is a fun thing to own.

Feasting

Feasting has been a part of Christmas festivities for centuries. Other customs such as the Christmas tree and the exchanging of gifts came later. When the Jamestown colonists arrived in Virginia they brought memories of roast goose, plum pudding, and the wassail bowl with them. As soon as they were sufficiently established, they began to recreate the Christmas celebrations with which they were familiar.

The settlers adapted native American foods which were abundant to make the Christmas treats we know today. Thus the wild turkey replaced the roast goose, and corn, sweet potatoes, and pumpkins accompanied the bird. The native oysters became popular, venison took the place of beef, and eventually when hogs were plentiful, ham was part of a Virginia Christmas menu.

Mince pies are said to go back to the Crusaders who brought back exotic spices from the East. They were a favorite in England for centuries where they were baked in rectangular form to represent the manger, Christ's cradle; the spices served as the offerings of the Wise men, according to one source.

The first mince meat made in Virginia probably used venison as a substitute for the British beef. Recipes appearing in old cookbooks gave detailed instructions for "mincing" the meat. The beef was cooked until it was very tender and could be cut into tiny pieces. To this beef suet was added, chopped apples, raisins, currants and a variety of spices: cinnamon, nutmeg, cloves, ginger, juice and grated rind of a lemon, sugar, apple cider or grape wine. One old recipe called for molasses and butter as well as suet. Today's cooks who serve mince meat pie probably buy a can from the supermarket and add some seasoning of their choice. This produces a pale imitation of homemade mince meat.

The queen of the holiday desserts in my childhood was the fruit cake. Rich, dark, moist and smelling of the variety of fruits which it contained, it was served with wine jelly or boiled custard as the perfect complement to a festive meal.

When I began housekeeping in 1937, the homemade fruit cake was traditional in my husband's family. In his eyes the family recipe was the "only fruit cake" so I set about mastering the process of preparing the ingredients, mixing and baking it.

My growing up had not included this activity. We always received a fruit cake from a city cousin; it was her one culinary accomplishment and was much prized by my mother. (As I remember, it was rather dry.)

The pre-Christmas ritual of making the family fruit cake was headed by my sister-in-law Lillian who kindly offered to help me make my first one. The process really required two days; one to prepare the ingredients and one to mix and bake. The English walnuts were shelled and cut into small pieces, citron, pineapple and candied cherries were cut up, flour and sugar were weighed and two boxes of raisins and two boxes of currants were soaked overnight in wine. The butter was put out to soften and the tube pans lined with greased brown paper cut to fit.

Next day the mixing began early. The butter was placed in a dish pan (no mixing bowl was large enough). Lil began to work the butter with her hand while I poured in sugar gradually as she mixed. Then one by one I dropped in the ten eggs. The mixture was becoming light and fluffy as she worked. By the time the flour had been added the heavy mass half-filled the pan. Now the raisins and currants which had been drained and squeezed dry were added; next I put in the floured nuts, citron, pineapple and cherries. The process had been going on for more than an hour and Lil was tired from handling the thick mixture.

At last we were ready to divide the dough among three pans. The largest would take at least three hours to cook, the smaller ones baked more quickly.

After the baking was completed, the cakes were cooled, taken from the pans and wrapped in cheesecloth. The last step was to pour wine over each one and store them in tins to ripen. We placed a few slices of raw apple in the tins to keep them moist.

The process was time-consuming but the cakes were good and I continued to follow the annual ritual for years. Apparently, fruit cakes became popular in the late 19th and early 20th centuries. Many old cookbooks gave recipes for a variety of cakes but no fruit cake.

Twentieth century cookbooks provide a number of recipes for fruit cakes. The *Encyclopedic Cookbook* published in 1948 contains seven. In addition uncooked fruit cakes are popular with modern housewives. Pound cake is one of the oldest cakes. It was made, as the name implies, with a pound each of butter, sugar, and flour and a dozen eggs. It contained no baking powder or milk. The secret of a good pound cake was the beating and the slow cooking. The texture was fine and close-grained and it kept well. These cakes were baked on the open hearth long before we had stoves. Recipes for pound cake abound today, but they have been modified for modern needs. One that I like is called the cold-oven pound cake, but aside from being a plain cake it is not much like the old-fashioned pound cake.

Wine jelly, a gelatin based dessert, was a Christmas favorite. Colored with red food coloring, it was not only pretty but good to serve with fruit cake or other sweets. Homemade grape or blackberry wine was used.

Boiled custard was another traditional accompaniment for cake, served in cups with a sprinkle of nutmeg. Many people liked to pour the custard over the jelly, a combination which I think takes away from both.

Christmas feasts today follow the traditional ones to a certain extent, but they have much more variety and emphasis on eye appeal is much greater. Decorated cookies, molded desserts and salads, sparkling drinks, and attractive appetizers, encourage hearty eating, but for sheer good eating few surpass the old fashioned cakes and pies of our forebears.

Recipes

Wine Jelly
1 pkg. (4 envelopes) unflavored gelatin
3 cups sugar
1 pt. boiling water
juice of 4 lemons
1 pt. of cold water
1 pt. sherry
dash of salt

Pour cold water over gelatin and allow to stand to soften. Add boiling water and sugar. Stir until completely dissolved. Add sherry, lemon juice, salt and red food coloring if desired. Chill until firm. Serve with whipped cream.

Boiled Custard
2 cups milk
4 egg yolks, dash of salt
1/2 cup sugar, 3/4 tsp. vanilla

Scald the milk in a double boiler. Add the eggs slightly beaten and the sugar. Cook stirring constantly until the mixture coats the spoon. It is important to keep the water just below boiling point to keep the mixture from curdling. Remove from the stove, and add the vanilla. Serve cold.

Work

Hand-Dug Wells

"Many people were still using hand-dug wells in the 1950s and '60s" said George (Nippy) Griffin of Topping. "I've dug many a one. Got $5.00 a foot. If the well was fifty feet deep that was a nice piece of change back then," he said laughing. "The deepest well I ever dug was eighty-five feet, but most didn't go that deep."

Asked to describe the procedure, he explained:

> I had two men working with me. We'd set up a tripod with a block and tackle over the spot where the well was to be; next I'd rough out a circle about 2½ feet in diameter, just big enough for me to dig in.
>
> When I got down two or three feet I'd fill a bucket with dirt and the men on the ground would haul it up, empty it, and send it back down. We kept this up until we struck water. Sometimes I'd strike it at twenty or twenty-five feet; lots of times I had to go deeper.
>
> After that I'd dig deeper sending up buckets of mud and water. Then the men would hitch the block and tackle to a wooden curbing made to fit the hole and lower it into the well and I'd slide it into place. Then I'd dig until it settled and was covered with two or three feet of water.
>
> Now the men would lower a section of pre-fab concrete about four feet in height to rest on the wooden curbing.
>
> The weight would force the wooden curbing deeper. We kept adding sections till we got to ground level.
>
> The water would have to settle and clear, but after that it was fit to drink. Years back they used brick curbing but that was before my time.

James Hugh Easton of Warner, now in his 80s, was digging wells before Griffin was born. The procedure was similar, but the pay was less.

"I got $2.00-$3.00 a foot in the beginning," he said. "After the wooden curbing was in place, I bricked it up inside and then laid bricks on it all the way to the top. It was close work down there. Bricks and mortar were lowered to me by block and tackle. It was easier when the molded curbing came into use," said Easton who also cleaned and repaired wells.

A good well was an asset and a matter of pride to the owner who might brag about the fact that his well had an abundant supply of good tasting water and never ran dry in periods of drought.

The mineral content of water was a factor of importance. Water with a high sulphur content might be objectionable to one not accustomed to it. "Hard" water contained mineral salts which did not combine readily with soap to form lather and made doing laundry more difficult. "Soft" water lacked mineral salts, had a pleasant taste and was easy to use.

"The methods of building wells in the 17th and 18th centuries varied depending upon the depth of the water-bearing strata and the geological character of the ground through which they dug" according to a Colonial Williamsburg publication.

In low-lying areas such as Mathews and lower Middlesex water could be struck often within twenty feet. The well-digger's work was highly specialized and not without danger from cave-ins. Early Tidewater wells were usually of brick construction, the bricks being laid from the bottom up.

Reconstructed well-heads add much to the charm and character of Colonial Williamsburg today although they no longer provide water. Abandoned well-shafts have proved to be rich repositories of archaeological information to researchers interested in colonial life.

Many of us can still remember drawing a bucket of water using a pulley and rope to bring it up from the depths. These wells were dug in the manner described by Griffin; then a tightly constructed well-deck was built with a waist-high boxing surrounding the opening. Over it was a frame from which hung a pulley fitted with enough rope to reach to water level and back. A heavy bucket was tied to the rope; when it was lowered into the water it sank and filled. It was raised by pulling hand over hand on the rope over the pulley until it reached the top and could be lifted out and emptied.

Providing water for the stock on a farm, for household needs and laundry was a sizable job which required muscular effort and stamina.

It would be hard to over-emphasize the importance of the well in civilization. In ancient times the location of a well determined settlements and trade routes. In this country digging a well was one of the first acts of colonizing because the water supply held equal importance with food and shelter.

Drilled wells and indoor plumbing have changed the daily chores of many households. In addition, water consumption has increased tremendously. So far the aquifer has supplied our needs but with increased population and demand the next century may see us securing water from a surface reservoir as do our urban neighbors.

Well-house with bucket and coconut shell dipper suspended from the pulley above the well opening at the home of Mr. and Mrs. Vernon Norris of Topping, Virginia.

The Blacksmith

Have you ever seen the sparks fly from a blacksmith's anvil? Some people will certainly remember this sight because sixty years ago there were many blacksmith shops in the Middle Peninsula counties. Today they are almost non-existent.

The smith's vocation was an important one in the days of the first colonists and every community had its smithy. Building a house required hand-forged nails, latches, hinges, and other iron items. The H and L hinges seen in many old homes are often used to date the building. Wooden shutters, closed during the day to keep out the heat, were kept open with wrought-iron devices fastened to the side of the house. Ornamental iron work appeared in fire screens, andirons, and railings.

More practical needs in the kitchen were served with fireplace cranes, spits, tongs, warming racks, and cooking utensils.

Farming implements such as the hoe, rake, ax, frow, and adz all came from the blacksmith's forge as well as hand tools.

By the 19th century, the blacksmith was kept busy repairing farming equipment and making new items. Wagon wheels had iron rims, axles broke and had to be repaired. Hames (iron pieces on the horse collar), singletrees, wagon tongues, and buggy shafts had iron parts. Horses and mules, which pulled the plow or wagon, had to be shod periodically. Trappers had the smith construct traps and oystermen required shaft-tongs. The smith's work was essential.

Even in the first quarter of this century, on almost any day, a small crowd could be found at the local blacksmith's shop: a farmer waiting to have his wagon wheel repaired, a fox hunter having new shoes put on his riding horse, an oysterman ordering new "patent tongs."

The tools of the blacksmith changed little during the centuries; the anvil, a huge block of iron or steel, the forge or furnace, the hammer and tongs were the essential equipment.

When the forge was red hot, the smith selected a piece of metal, perhaps for a horse shoe, and using the long-handled tongs thrust it deep into the blaze to make it soft enough to shape. He then took it quickly to the anvil and began to flatten and bend the iron with blows of the hammer, the flying sparks falling harmlessly around him. The metal cooled quickly and had to be returned to the flame, then back to the anvil for more shaping. When the piece was ready, he plunged it into a tub of water to harden and set the metal. The whole operation took less than ten minutes.

L. J. (Joe) Pierce had a large blacksmith and feed business in Urbanna which he started in 1913.

"My father was a real artist with hot metal and he loved it," said Lewis W. Pierce, his son who still lives in Urbanna. "I used to help him some and I even got to be a pretty good welder" he continued.

"He did a lot of boat work, making rudders and propellers, and he made shaft and patent tongs for oystermen too.

"He had two anvils and two forges and every kind of tool you could think of: tongs, pliers and vises in different sizes. The forge was heated with coal," said Pierce. "It was real fine, called blacksmith's coal, and had to be ordered out of Baltimore. The coal and metal came down on the steamboat to Burton's Wharf."

Asked about the forging process, Pierce said his father used borax on the metal before putting it in the water to set it.

As many of the iron pieces once forged by the smith became available commercially, his skills, less in demand, were applied in new areas.

In 1900 R. M. Clements and Bro. advertised in the Southside Sentinel as blacksmiths, and wagon and carriage builders. Their ad also offered "a full line of burial caskets and coffins and a hearse provided on short notice." These services continued until about 1930. A similar shop in Deltaville served the same dual purpose.

By mid-century mortuary services were provided by undertakers and embalmers, farming had become almost entirely mechanized, and the blacksmith shop as a service disappeared.

Horses are still popular animals, however, and require the attention once provided by the local blacksmith.

Charley Brown of B-Bar-B Ranch at Glenns says he shoes his horses himself. "Occasionally I'm asked to put corrective shoes on a horse whose hooves have been split or damaged," he said.

"Now shoes can be purchased in different sizes and made to fit with a minimum of shaping.

"The old method of heating the metal had shaping it on an anvil is about gone," said Brown. "Tony Harper at Bena is the only man I know still doing it that way."

Pony and horse farms today usually depend upon a farrier who comes to the farm to do the trimming and shoeing of the animals. Such specialized services are far removed from the broad variety of skills employed by the smiths of earlier times.

Blacksmith Shop, c. 1920, Deltaville, Virginia.
Photo Courtesy of Dorothy Norris.

Grist Mills

Mills, milling, and millers! What contributions each has made to the economic history of Virginia! Even though few mills remain in operation today, the name mill appears in place names, the surname Miller fills pages in the telephone book, and millponds still add beauty to the landscape here and there.

The mill site has always been a romantic setting; the sound of the rushing water turning the ponderous mill wheel, the clatter of the machinery when grinding was in progress, and even the miller himself white with the dust of flour, all are picturesque and memorable images.

Corbin's Mill, which once stood on Route 14 in lower King and Queen County, was typical of watermills erected by colonial plantation owners. It was part of the holdings of Richard Corbin, one of the richest men of his time. Plantation owners erected mills to grind corn and wheat for their own use, feeding family members, indentured servants and slaves. As a convenience for neighboring small farmers, the owner ground their grain exacting a toll for the service.

These mills operated by a wheel which turned as water from the pond, conducted through a spillway, rushed into the huge troughs located along its rim. Made of oak and standing twelve feet or more in diameter, the wheel drove the upper millstone causing it to rotate against the nether stone which was stationary. Grain passed between the stones to be ground into a fine powder. The degree of fineness or coarseness of the product was controlled by adjusting the distance between the revolving stone.

The building housing the machinery was usually three stories in height to provide space for the elevators which transported the flour to the upper floor to be sieved. Passing downward through the sieves, it was separated into three grades: flour, seconds, and grudgings, a coarse mixture containing the husks of the wheat.

John Garrett, who lived in the vicinity of Corbin's Mill, had vivid memories of the mill house, the machinery, and the millers. "The mill ground six days a week and its patronage was so heavy, people often had to leave their corn to be ground later at the miller's convenience," he recalled. "Grinding wore down the stones and they had to be dressed every few weeks," Garrett continued. He smiled as he remembered the scene:

> I've seen Forest Norman dress those stones many a time. He used a kind of pick: I think they called it a "millbill." Funny looking little tool. He'd sit there all day pecking at those stones to make them rough. When they got smooth they didn't grind proper.
>
> He used to wear goggles to protect his eyes from the fragments of stone and bits of metal that flew off the pick as he worked. It was slow work because the stones were so big. As I remember they were about five feet in diameter. The top stone was maybe ten to twelve inches thick, the bottom one was thinner.

Millstones were imported for the earliest mills. French burr stones were considered best, but others came from the Rhine area of Germany. Later stones quarried in Virginia or North Carolina came into use.

The first colonists at Jamestown brought wheat for planting with the expectation of erecting mills for grinding it. However, defense against the Indians became top priority, and the hungry settlers were forced to trade with the Indians for maize (corn). This grain, unknown to the Englishmen then, eventually became a subsistence crop.

The first grain mill in the colony was actually a windmill built by Governor Yeardley on his plantation at the falls of the James River. By 1649 in Virginia there were nine mills in operation: four windmills and five watermills. Today a faithfully constructed windmill exists to grind corn in Colonial Williamsburg. Watermills became more numerous in the Tidewater area. Some were tide mills powered by the flow of the tide.

A tide mill still stands at Poplar Grove on the East River in Mathews County. Said to have ground corn for General George Washington's troops during the siege of Yorktown, it could grind up to thirty-two bushels of corn on one tide. It was burnt by Federal soldiers during the Civil War but was rebuilt and operated until 1912. Today its significance is recognized by its place on the Historic Landmarks Register.

Prosperous mill owners eventually produced meal and flour for export. George Washington, Robert Carter, and William Byrd II, all operated mills for commercial purposes. Before the Revolution a thriving trade existed with the West Indies. Later, mills in the United States produced flour for ship supplies and for the growing city markets.

Good millers were always in demand. Beginning in colonial times, legislation was enacted to prevent the taking of excessive tolls, however. The importance of the miller's work was shown in his being exempt from military service. In fact, he could be fined as much as 100 pounds of tobacco if he even appeared at a regimental muster because these events often turned into bouts of revelry which might prevent the miller from performing his regular duties at the mill.

Corbin's Mill was only one of many King and Queen County mills. Others were Walkerton Mill, its pond still a place of quiet beauty; Canterbury Mill on the Mattaponi River, and Trice's near Mascot.

In Middlesex County two ponds remain to recall the ancient water mills. Hilliard's Mill on Route 602 between Urbanna and Churchview was operating in 1715, its name changing with successive owners. Healy's Mill on Route 629 ceased operation when the dam broke in the 1930's.

John R. Brooke of Saluda whose grandfather was Jimmy Thurston, one of the last millers at Corbin's Mill, tells this story:

> After the dam burst at Healy's the mill was washed away. It may have been in the storm of 1933 when so much damage was caused, I'm not sure. Some years later Granddaddy and Daddy searched the woods there and found the millstones. I was a small boy but they took me with them. I remember the stones were nearly covered with

vines and brush. Granddaddy bought them and had them hauled to Corbin's to replace the ones there.

He thought for a minute before continuing.

> I loved to go to Corbin's Mill. Granddaddy would let me play there until the mill was running, but then I had to leave. Too dangerous, he said. After the stones were replaced, it ran a few more years; then it stopped for good. A pity! I loved the old mill.

A colorful part of American life passed with the closing of the mills but the ponds, reminders of their existence, still give beauty to local roadsides.

Wilton Mill, Middlesex County, Virginia.
This mill produced water-ground flour and corn meal.
Photo courtesy of Violene Jackson.

The Versatile Apple

Apples have always been big in Virginia where the first settlers found crabapples growing in abundance. To this native stock the colonists grafted apple branches brought from England. Plantation owners, attempting to make their estates as self-sufficient as possible, planted large orchards and small landowners set out a few trees as well. Apples, pears, peaches, and cherries provided fruit in season and could be carried over for winter use in some form. Among these fruits the apple was the most versatile.

Housewives dried apples, made apple butter and apple jelly, but cider-making was perhaps the most important to the Colonial household because cider was a drink for year round use. Coffee served in private homes was unusual in the 17th century and tea was expensive, but cider could be made of home grown apples and stored in quantity.

The early cider mill or cider press was not a complicated machine. Unskilled labor could turn the bountiful apple crop into a potable drink for general use. Apples which had been stored for a few weeks made the best cider. They were washed, fed into the mill and ground to a pulp releasing an amber juice. It could be kept fresh for only a short period before it began to ferment and became hard cider.

The season for cider-making in the late fall became a time of merry-making. Visitors were freely treated to the tangy drink and soon became "very merry." Although the alcoholic content is not considered high it soon showed its effects.

William Byrd jotted in his diary an incident which occurred in Williamsburg in 1709. "We drank some of Will Robinson's cider till we were all very merry and then went by the coffee-house and pulled poor Col. Churchill out of bed." Pranks, apparently, have always appealed to the young.

In the 18th century a visitor to Middlesex recounted a social occasion where "a considerable company of people gathered for the purpose of drinking cider and dancing. Without [doors] the tankard went round and round while the sound of music was heard within."

Taverns and inns served cider as an accompaniment to meals but as a drink on order as well.

Cider was also used occasionally as a form of payment in lieu of tobacco. An instance is on record where a mother contracted with a teacher to "Learne my children two years and take cider from learning them at 6d per gallon." A shilling then was about five cents.

Cider or beer was served to laborers in the fields who thought it would ward off malaria. A farmer who could provide only water to the hired help was considered poor indeed. No wonder that apple trees were everywhere and apple products so popular.

Could it be that the adage; "an apple a day keeps the doctor away" derived from this supposed cure for malaria?

Apple cider was no less popular in New England. Apples flourish in temperate climates, so from Maine to the Carolinas apples and their juices were popular. John Adams, second president of the United States, is said to have consumed a tankard of cider with his breakfast up to the time of his death at age 91. Quite a testimonial for the health giving qualities of the apple.

Apples and peaches spread west with the pioneers. John Chapmen (1775-1845), better known as Johnny Appleseed, is credited with propagating the Midwest with apples. He is said to have visited the cider-presses of his neighbors and collected apple seeds which he sowed in clearings as he traveled west.

When the seedlings were large enough to transplant, anyone who wished could take one to plant at his homestead.

Peaches are said to have been carried west in the same way. Settlers threw the pits in fertile spots. Perhaps these planters envisioned a future source of peach brandy as a welcome change from cider.

Cider today is enjoyed in season, available at roadside stands and farmers' markets, but its use is short lived. Few people in the Middle Peninsula bother to make cider.

However, John and Violet Brooke of Saluda make gallons of apple juice every fall giving most of it away. None of it becomes hard cider. The process is simple. Apples are fed into the mill, ground to a pulp, the juice collected in buckets, the pulp fed to the cattle. Strained, the pale juice, with no additives, is bottled in plastic milk jugs and frozen. All that is needed is to thaw it and it is ready to drink: Delicious . . . Healthy . . . Inexpensive . . . Convenient!

A by-product of apple cider is vinegar. For centuries some people produced good quality vinegar with an acidity level high enough to keep pickle. According to Jim Morse of Mad Maggie's Fruit Farm, in Middlesex, cider changes to vinegar when kept at higher temperatures. The natural yeast which feeds on the sugar content of the apple juice causes fermentation which continues until it produces vinegar. This yeast colony forms a large gelatin-like mass known as "mother" which eventually settles to the bottom of the keg or barrel and does not affect the clarity of the product. Commercial vinegars carry a label guaranteeing an acidity of five percent. Home producers of vinegar seldom knew the actual acidity level, but if it kept pickle it was good enough.

Vinegar is used as a condiment today, but until modern times it had cosmetic uses as the basis for body lotions. It was also a good cleaning agent for household use.

The apple, if indeed it was the fruit of the Tree of Knowledge which Eve gave to Adam, has proved a blessing to man in many forms. Bite into a crisp Golden Delicious and reflect upon the history and the uses of the apple from the era of pre-history until today. Apple growing in Virginia is still a major industry and apple eating is a healthful practice.

Making Sorghum Molasses

A ritual of fall which I still miss is the making of sorghum molasses. The mingled scent of wood smoke and boiling cane syrup and the picture of the horse plodding in endless circles around the mill were colorful accents to a crisp autumn day.

Molasses Mill. Photo by Forrest W. Patton, courtesy of Robert R. Harper

Sorghum, a relative of sugar cane, was widely grown in Tidewater Virginia for the delicious molasses which formed a staple of diet on most farms. These who did not cultivate a crop bought a few gallons of molasses from those who did.

The molasses pitcher was put on the table at each meal along with the butter, cream and sugar. Breakfast usually ended with one or two hot biscuits and molasses and also other meals if dessert was not provided. Molasses made delicious cookies and gingerbread, or molasses pudding. Served warm with lemon sauce it was a company dessert; cold with a glass of milk, it was a wonderful after school snack.

Molasses was the main ingredient for candy-pulling, once a popular social activity for young people. Molasses would be cooked down to a very thick syrup, then poured into a buttered dish or pan. When it was cool enough to handle, the mass was rolled into a ball, then pulled out into a heavy rope.

A boy and girl with buttered hands would pull it back and forth as far as it would stretch. After five or ten minutes the candy would change color to a rich golden shade. When it became too hard to pull it was laid out in a long rope to cool completely and then broken into bite-sized pieces.

The cane was planted in late May or early June. The seeds produced handsome plants which resembled corn except that they grew ten to twelve feet tall with a cluster of seeds at the top which turned dark red and attracted blackbirds and crows.

Sorghum, harvested just before frost, was grown for the juice extracted from the stalks. Someone who owned a sorghum mill would appear to grind the stalks and cook the syrup for a toll of the crop.

The mill consisted of three rollers and it was operated by a horse hitched to a long pole, or sweep, which turned the rollers as it walked around the mill in a circle. The stalks were fed into the mill and crushed between the rollers. A bright green juice ran from the crushed stalks. It was strained through several layers of cloth as it ran into a barrel.

When enough juice had collected to make a batch of molasses, the cooking began. The boiler, or evaporator, was an open, shallow, galvanized pan about four by eight feet long and six inches deep. A fire was built under the pan and kept burning during the process.

As soon as the watery juice began to boil a dark foam appeared on top. This had to be skimmed off with a handmade strainer. The stirring, cooking, and skimming went on for three or four hours with a man constantly in attendance to keep the fire burning and to see that the syrup did not burn as it thickened. It was, therefore, important to control the heat; too hot a fire might scorch the syrup or overcook it. At last the man cooking the syrup would begin to test it to see if it was the right consistency. If not cooked enough it would be "runny."

The syrup thickened as it cooled. If it was thick when it was hot, in winter it would be almost semi-solid. "Slow as cold molasses in the winter-time" was a homely comparison understood by anyone who had ever waited for the syrup to pour from a barrel or even a molasses pitcher on a cold morning.

It is said that molasses was once even sold in a paper bag at the grocery stores; in its semi-solid state it was carried home without difficulty.

When the syrup had been cooked to the peak of perfection, it was thick, amber, shining and smelled delicious.

The average farmer paid the operator of the mill one gallon for every four gallons which had been made. For his own use he kept a sufficient quantity to meet the needs of his family and sold the remainder.

Few people in eastern Virginia grow or mill sorghum today. Latane Trice of Walkerton acquired an old sorghum mill a few years ago and with some difficulty found parts to put it in working condition. With even more difficulty, he found seeds to raise a crop of sorghum! Apparently moved by nostalgia, he grew the cane, used the mill to crush the stalks and cooked the syrup to his satisfaction. The product was up to standard and his old friends, I among them, enjoyed the rare treat of King & Queen homemade molasses. However, I believe he did not mill a second crop. Commercial products are easily available but do not compare with the "real stuff."

Whitewash, the Poor Man's Paint

"Too poor to paint and too proud to white wash" was a saying popular around the turn of the century. Prosperous homeowners had abandoned whitewash, the old-fashioned and economical method of refurbishing their buildings, for the more expensive but longer lasting paint, which had become a status symbol of sorts.

Whitewashing in Virginia goes back to Colonial days when it was in common use to combat mildew, so ever-present in warm, damp climates. It was used inside as well as on exterior surfaces just as it had been in the thatched cottages of the settlers' native England.

An advantage of whitewash, in addition to its cheapness, was that it required no expertise to apply. It went on easily, dried quickly, and produced a brilliant white surface. A coarse brush, a bucket of whitewash and a youngster to apply it could change the looks of a fence in a hurry. Mark Twain's classic account of how Tom Sawyer whitewashed a fence is known to most of us, but often little else is known today of this product.

Nevertheless, the term "to whitewash" has become a part of the language. In Webster's dictionary one of the meanings given is "to gloss over or to conceal faults." Many people use the expression "a whitewash job" meaning giving a false impression or hiding faults. The origin of the term goes back to the capacity of whitewash to hide defects and give an attractive appearance.

Whitewashing was once a standard practice in rural homes. Its main ingredient, lime, had other uses and was purchased by the sack and kept on hand. One use was as a disinfectant to disguise unpleasant odors; another was as an insect repellent. It was an ingredient in food for cattle and poultry also. Perhaps the most important use was to counteract acidity in the soil. Agricultural lime is still widely used by farmers though newer preparations have replaced its other uses.

A spring ritual which I remember well was whitewashing the out buildings and fences at my home. The hired boy (usually a youngster twelve to fourteen years old) would be set to work on this job because it was easy and less risky than whitewashing a larger building which might require a tall ladder.

The first task was to prepare the surface to be whitewashed which meant scraping off loose bits left from previous coats. A wire brush or a stiff broom was all that was needed for this step.

Next, the whitewash had to be made. A wash tub was sunk in the ground a few inches by digging a shallow hole the size of the tub and piling the earth around it. Then the lime was put in the tub and a bucket of well water was poured over it. The chemical reaction was exciting.

Seated on top of a nearby fence where I could see it all, I watched the mass boil up emitting clouds of steam. The person preparing the whitewash used a hoe with a long handle to stir it, carefully avoiding the boiling which shook the tub in its intensity. After it had cooled, the painter would add more water continuing to stir until it was thin enough to spread easily. If the mixture was too thick it flaked off when dry.

The brush used for applying whitewash was coarse and quite unlike a paintbrush. It was sold without a handle so that the user had to construct one to fit the holes in the wooden frame. Sometimes this was an old broom stick whittled to fit.

"Now, Willie," my father would say, "I want you to start with this hen house until you get the hang of it. Then you can do the fences and last the smoke house. You'll have to use a ladder for that and if you're afraid, I'll get Charles Simmons to do it."

Willie would set to work splashing white wash from a dripping brush and covering the ground around the building.

"Don't dip your brush all the way to the bottom of the bucket," my father would instruct. "Keep a stick to stir it up and let your brush drip a little before you begin," he would say.

I would watch until Willie got the hang of it and was doing a good job, then losing interest I would find something else to do. By lunch time Willie would have finished the hen house and be ready for the next job. When all the outbuildings had received attention, the improvement was almost miraculous. Dingy, faded weather boarding would sparkle in the sunlight, defects hidden for the time at least.

Arthur Robins, who owned and operated Middlesex Farm Supply for many years, said at one time demand for hydrated or air-slaked lime, was steady, but now it is stocked only in small quantities.

"I've used plenty of it when I was growing up," Arthur remembers. "Everybody did, but today it's different. Not many people bother to do things like we did back in the '30s and '40s."

Instructions for preparing whitewash can be secured from the Virginia Cooperative Extension Service. Directions for preparing the surface, mixing, and cleaning up are explicit. Directions for producing various tints for interior work are also included. Many people, in my day, preferred to purchase calcimine, a ready-mixed preparation, already tinted. It had to be mixed with water and applied with a finer brush than whitewash. Sears, Roebuck offered them in 1902 for as low as 68 cents each.

Apparently whitewashing as a quick, easy, inexpensive method of improving the appearance of buildings has not disappeared entirely. However, it has been a long time since I've seen a boy whitewashing a fence.

Lumbering 1910-1918

The soil of King and Queen County is particularly well-suited to the growth of soft woods—loblolly and spruce pine—and a variety of hardwoods such as oak, poplar, and gum. In the early decades of the twentieth century our rich timberlands began to attract outside business interests. By 1910 timberland was selling for $3.00 to $5.00 per acre, the land owners finding the money for the land more attractive than the money-making trees thereon. Deed Book records in the court house record many transactions at this price.

Recognizing the value of the great tracts of untouched timber and the low prices prevailing at the time, businessmen such as George Bradley, Bill Morris, Jim Coulbourn, Henry Vandalia Perry and sons from Maryland and W. G. Beane, Jr., Herbert Hall and his brother Frank from Northern Neck began buying timber in the vicinity of King and Queen C. H. for the purpose of producing rough lumber for market. The Mattaponi River with deep-water landings such as Mantapike, Court House, Melrose, and Clifton provided convenient locations where vessels could be loaded.

The operation of sawmills at this time required crews of from ten to fifteen men to cut, log, and to run the mill itself as well as to haul the rough lumber to the landings. In order to insure a steady labor supply the mill owners constructed lumber camps near the mill site to house the workers needed although men living nearby walked to work. These shanties were approximately twelve feet long by eight feet wide. Bunks made of rough lumber nailed against the wall with wood slats to support mattresses filled with wheat straw or even pine needles constituted sleeping arrangements. Wood heaters furnished heat in these make-shift dormitories and lanterns or oil lamps gave light. A wash basin which hung on a nail outside the shanty door was used by all the men for what ablutions they thought necessary.

A separate shack housed the kitchen with an iron wood-burning range for preparation of meals. One of the men was cook. Breakfast was usually salt herring, fatback, biscuits, and coffee or tea. Lunch was invariable beans which had been cooking all morning on the old range with fatback and cornbread. The evening meal was slightly more varied: fatback, vegetables such as black eye peas, turnips, cabbage, tomatoes, and sweet potatoes; dried fruit such as prunes and peaches; and generous quantities of bread. Salmon cakes were a real treat when they occasionally appeared on the menu. One staple at every meal was sorghum or black strap molasses. The fare, though plain and lacking in variety, was abundant. It is told that cabbage was cooked in a lard tin to satisfy the hearty appetites of the hard-working men.

The work week was from Monday until mid-day Saturday. The men apparently enjoyed camp life. At night some played cards by the light of the lantern and they told stories of their exploits in the woods. Laughter and singing were rich and spontaneous. Luther Muse, who remembers those days, said that he could count the stars through the cracks in the shanty, but he never even had a cold, and sickness was rare among the workers.

The camp not only housed the men who worked the mill, but it also stabled the horses, mules, and oxen needed in the logging operation. A good water supply was, therefore, a necessity. If a spring was not available, a well had to be dug at each location. Water was needed to fill the boiler of the steam engine which provided power to run the mill and to supply the animals as well as the men. When the camp moved on to a new site the well was covered over with slabs or logs to protect hunters or animals from inadvertently falling into it. Seldom were these wells actually filled. Abandoned wells can be found today in cut-over land where the unfilled holes are hazards to the unwary.

W. G. Beane owned two such camps and Bird and Allen, a business partnership between Spotswood Bird and Roland Allen, owned one.

Work in the woods required brawn and stamina. The day began at sunup and often continued until sundown with an hour's rest at midday. Wages were low; men earned from $1.00 to $1.25 per day. At Beane's mills the workers were paid by check, but at some other mills they received a due bill in lieu of wages which could be redeemed for groceries at the store run by Bird and Allen or at C. C. Vaughan's of Cumnor. Men would bring their time (hours worked) to the store to be paid in food. Little money changed hands. This means of payment was a kind of barter system which seemed satisfactory to both employer and employee.

Lumbering methods at this time were in sharp contrast to those in use today. Trees were sawed by hand. Two men wielding a crosscut saw could bring down a tree of average size in a relatively short time. The saw partners who cut together established a rhythmic motion as they pulled the long saw back and forth across the grain of the tree to fell it. W. S. Beane, who as a boy was often at his father's mill, says there were two motions used. One called "the cha-cha" was a series of short even strokes; the other called "the hell bottom" was a long stroke with a snatch at the end. The men knew the exact type of stroke needed in each situation. Large trees with diameters from two to three feet were not uncommon. Such trees required extra attention to cut them to fall free (in the clear) to avoid hanging against other trees and damaging all. Once on the ground, the limbs of the trees had to be lopped off and the trunks cut into lengths of eight, ten, or twelve feet before the logs could be brought to the mill.

Before moving them to the mill shed, the logs were first drawn into piles using "grabs" (hooks somewhat like huge ice tongs). The grabs had a large ring through which passed a heavy chain to which a horse was hitched. The horse was often so well-trained that it seemed to know instinctively where the next logs were to go in the pile. The logs formed a pyramid-like pile four feet wide at the base and 3½ feet in height and were secured by a heavy chain. Then a two-wheeled trip-cart pulled by horses or mules was backed over the pile and the load was suspended under the cart by using an ingenious device like a huge lever to lift the heavy logs clear of the ground.

In difficult terrain such as hillsides or gullies an ox cart was used. This was a special very heavy two-wheeled cart drawn by a team of oxen, perhaps the most powerful beasts of burden. Ponderous and stolid, the oxen were driven without lines. They responded to the special language of the driver. To his call of "byak" they turned to the right, "yea" to the left, and his deep-throated shout, "whoa" brought them to a stop. The driver also used a long rawhide whip which he flicked over their backs and horns to make them back.

The mill itself required six or eight men to operate it: the fireman, the log turner, the sawyer, the off-bearer and a man in the dust hole who carried off the sawdust in a wheel barrow. Another man took slabs to the slab pit and burned them. It took two men to run the edger which trimmed the boards to size. Chief among the mill hands was the sawyer whose job involved both risk and responsibility and who earned slightly higher wages. Thomas H. Watkins was sawyer and foreman at one of Beane's mills and Bob Shackleford held a similar position at the other. From $6.00 a week a sawyer's wage advanced to the princely sum of $10.00 weekly after World War I when all wages began to rise.

There were men whose specialty was logging and others who excelled with the cross cut saw. On a frosty morning it was not unusual to see a mill hand with his saw on his shoulder, the sun glinting on its polished surface as he strode toward the mill for his day's work. Occasionally the ox cart with its driver perched precariously on its frame would be seen lumbering toward the mill.

Hauling the sawed timber to the landing required other workers. After the logs had been sawed the lumber was hacked up on the lumber yard to dry. When the curing process was complete, it was hauled to the landing to await a vessel to transport it to market. During the slack season on the farm, some farmers would use their wagons and team to haul lumber. Among these were Alex Oliver, John B. Jeffries, Melvin Carlton, and Herbert Ball. They were paid by the 1000 feet to haul from the mill yard to the landing.

Vessels such as the *John R. P. Moore*, the *L. E. Williams*, and the *Blackbird* were used regularly by the lumberman to transport lumber. When vessels sailed up the river to drop anchor at Melrose or Court House Landing, it was a time of activity and excitement. They could carry in their holds and on deck from 100,000-125,000 board feet of rough lumber at a trip, and loading provided local men another opportunity to earn a few dollars. When a vessel arrived it was riding high in the water with an empty hold; it departed heavy with cargo, making its way slowly and majestically down the Mattaponi, to enter the York and thence into the Chesapeake Bay bound for Baltimore, the market for most of the lumber shipped from King and Queen.

Among the captains that W. S. Beane recalls are Capt. Lee and Capt. John Insley, who at one time or another captained all of the vessels mentioned.

Sawmills in the early twentieth century made an important contribution to the economy of King and Queen and the surrounding counties at a time when work was scarce and money was hard to come by. With the close of World War I came changes that brought an end to this colorful period. The thump of the axe, the rasp of the saw, the shouts of men in the woods, the whine of the saw as it bit into a log, and the singing of the men at night in the shanties, such sounds would be heard no more. Gone too were the flap of the sails of the *Blackbird* and the creak of her rigging as she slipped quietly down the river toward the bay.

Commerce on the Rappahannock

There have always been boats upon the Rappahannock River. First, the Indian dugout canoes, later the sailing vessels of the white man, followed by mechanized crafts of many kinds.

Capt. John Smith was the first Englishman to reach the falls of the river when in 1608 he and a few companions rowed and sailed an open boat up many Chesapeake Bay tributaries exploring and mapping the new country.

Perhaps the earliest commercial traffic on the river was that of the fur traders who sailed their shallops far up these rivers to reach Indian villages in search of furs.

"An Act for erecting a town in Spotsylvania County" (1727) stated that there was increasing need for public landings and wharves to accommodate the flourishing tobacco trade as one reason for establishing the town which became Fredericksburg. The river was said to be a half mile wide and to have a depth of twelve feet with a normal tide rise of four feet, which was sufficient for most sea-going vessels at that time.

During the late 18th century a tremendous trade was carried on by top-sails and sloops with New England, the West Indies, and British ports. They imported all types of commodities and exported corn, wheat, flour and tobacco as well as other products in large quantities.

By early 19th century with the advent of the steamboat which transported live cargo and fresh foods, much of the other commercial traffic was being handled by two and three-masted schooners. The burgeoning lumber industry provided ample cargo.

Capt. Willis Cannon of Urbanna remembers sailing on the *Mannaway* owned by J. W. Hurley and on the *Kate W. Tilghman* owned by Otho Smith, both of Urbanna. These schooners hauled wood products such as cord wood, pulp wood, and logs. They picked up cargo at landings on both the North and South sides of the river. Stevedores loaded and off-loaded the cargo at its destination, usually Baltimore.

Sailing vessels gradually disappeared from the river following World War II and manned barges took their place. The Eastern Transportation Company of Baltimore operated a fleet of barges, some 125-175 feet long. A single tug towed several barges hooked one behind the other. They had a cabin and galley and the captain often had his wife and children along. She did the cooking and he operated the barge.

Oil tankers were common sights on the river during the first half of this century when oil products were in great demand. This traffic ended with the establishment of the oil pipeline which made overland transportation quicker and more convenient.

Today, commercial traffic on the river is largely confined to barges belonging to the Chesapeake Corporation of Virginia, which picks up pulpwood at designated landings and transports it to the mill at West Point.

"The river is dying," said Capt. Cannon. "Silting and erosion have filled in the channel at Fredericksburg so that only shallow draft boats can go in. The old docks are gone. There's nothing there now but some piling to show where a thriving port once existed.

"Pleasure boats are all you see on the river now," he finished sadly remembering the busy thoroughfare which once was the Rappahannock.

Church and School

Christ Episcopal Church, Mathews

Some churches refuse to die. Fortunately a number of colonial churches in our area serve as landmarks today attesting to the truth of this statement. Such a one is Christ Episcopal Church, Kingston Parish, in Mathews County. The present building is possibly the fourth church on that site.

Kingston Parish was one of four parishes in Colonial Gloucester County. The others are Petsworth, Ware, and Abingdon; all were in existence in the latter half of the 17th century.

When in 1791 Mathews County separated from Gloucester to become a new governmental entity, its boundaries followed those of the parish and remain so today.

Settlements in Gloucester began as early as 1649 and it is highly probable that some type of house of worship soon followed; however, extant Kingston Parish church records begin in 1679. Two vestry books survive. The second begins in 1740 and continues to 1796 showing that the church survived the Revolutionary War when many did not.

In the Colonial period it was customary to establish chapels at various locations for the convenience of communicants. North River Chapel was located between the North River and Blackwater Creek. Chapel of Hesse stood near the head of Queen Creek. Local names such as Chapel Creek and Chapel Neck are reminders of the existence of these buildings.

The Revolutionary War wrought havoc on the Church of England congregations and buildings. Many lost members, fell into disrepair, and eventually ceased to exist. Some buildings were acquired by other denominations. For instance, in King and Queen County the church of Stratton Major Parish at

Shanghai was purchased by the United Methodist Church and at Cumnor, Mattaponi, which had stood empty for years, came into the hands of a Baptist congregation. This was not the case with Christ Church of Kingston Parish. Although it suffered through many difficulties, it never lost its identity.

In 1785 it made the transition from the Anglican or Church of England to the Protestant Episcopal Church of the United States and continued under the new designation with a new vestry after ties with the mother country had been severed.

By early 19th century, however, the church was without a rector for long periods, the building had fallen into great disrepair, and both chapels had disappeared. According to church records, it was revived and restored largely through the efforts of Elizabeth Tompkins, sister of Capt. Sally Tompkins, CSA. The sisters are buried in the cemetery, their stones among the earliest identifiable graves.

Christ Church was burned in 1904, the fire caused by the igniting of Christmas decorations. The present building was erected in 1906. It was built of local materials and the bricks salvaged from the ruins. The late Milton Murray is credited for the new building.

A church history prepared by Kingston Parish states: "It is believed that the church was at one time cruciform, or shaped like a cross, as neighboring Abingdon in Gloucester and Christ Church in Lancaster still are today. . . . Limited explorations of the area indicate it may be so."

The present building is laid in American bond. It has a parquet oak ceiling ornamented with wooden pendants in the shape of acorns. The origin of the chandelier, once lighted by kerosene lanterns, is uncertain, but it adds a Victorian touch to the edifice.

The new parish house, which replaced an earlier one, was dedicated in 1987. Christ Church is in a thriving condition today with an active congregation.

Trinity Church at Foster dates from 1854. It served originally as the church for the western part of the parish while Christ Church served the eastern. In recent years an attempt to merge the two congregations was made. However, services were restored at Trinity. Today it draws communicants from a wide area offering the traditional Anglican service.

Christ Church, Kingston Parish, Mathews County.

An Early Baptist Church

Lower King and Queen Baptist Church, constituted in 1772 by John Waller, is the oldest Baptist church in the county and one of the oldest in Virginia. However, Glebe Landing Baptist Church in Middlesex County was constituted on the same date and shares the same distinction for Middlesex.

The Baptist movement first gained a foothold in Virginia in Orange and Spotsylvania Counties and spread eastward rapidly. John Waller, pastor of Lower Spotsylvania Baptist Church and a zealous and courageous preacher, visited Essex, Middlesex and King and Queen in 1770 preaching in various localities. The following year, together with Robert Ware and William Weber, he returned meeting with strong opposition from the Established Church. In fact, the three were imprisoned for preaching without a license and spent forty-six days in the jail in Urbanna where they continued to preach from the windows to large crowds gathered outside.

By the time of their return in 1772 the opposition had subsided and the two churches were formed without further difficulty.

The first "meeting house" for the King and Queen congregation is believed to have been a log structure located perhaps a half mile from the present site.

Robert Ware, one of the three jailed in 1771, became its first pastor, a tenure that lasted thirty-one years and gave rise to the local name "Wares" by which it is unofficially known today.

In 1834 a modest brick building was erected. Rectangular in shape with a sharply peaked roof, it was laid in Flemish bond. A stoop protected the entrance which opened into a small vestibule. Galleries for the black members extended around three sides. No provision for heat was made in the original building. Later two large stoves with pipes supported by wires led to a central chimney on the roof.

This building burned on Sunday, February 2, 1919. A light snow had fallen the previous night and the attendance was small on this winter day. The roof was ablaze before the worshipers knew that the building was on fire.

There was absolutely no means of fighting the fire. The supply of water consisted of a single bucket of drinking water in the vestibule, there was no well on the property, and the spring was some distance away. There were no ladders to reach the flaming roof, no fire company to call or telephone to use. Realizing the futility of trying to put out the fire, the members concentrated their efforts on saving the contents of the building. Virtually all the furnishings were saved including the benches and carpet.

Plans to rebuild were quickly begun and in May 1921 the present commodious frame building, constructed on the same site, was dedicated with appropriate ceremonies. The following year the 150th anniversary of the church was celebrated in the new building.

Extant records of the church begin in 1843 with a minute book now kept in the archives of the Virginia Baptist Historical Society. The membership roster for that year listed 118 white members, 115 black, and 31 "free colored" making a grand total of 264. There were six deacons, three of which were black.

A mother church, Lower King and Queen claims four daughters. The first of these is Poroporone which became an independent entity in 1808. Mattaponi, the second daughter, was established in 1828 and Olivet, the third, in 1842.

Following the Civil War, the black members withdrew, and with the assistance and blessing of the mother church, established the flourishing church known today as Second Mt. Olive located near Truhart, thus becoming the fourth and last daughter church.

During the Civil War years the church minutes make no reference to the agonizing struggle going on in the South.

However, church business meetings were held irregularly and offerings were smaller although it appears that services continued to be held on Sunday.

In 1872 the church celebrated its Centennial. Up to that time it had had only three pastors: Robert Ware, 31 years, William Todd, 52 years and Isaac Diggs, 17 years.

Lower King and Queen draws its membership from a wide area. Some trace their church ancestry back to grandparents and even great-grandparents.

Now well into its third century of service to God, the church celebrated its 220th anniversary on October 11, 1992, with the traditional morning and afternoon services and a mid-day dinner on the grounds.

Revivals

In the 1920s August was the month when many rural Baptist churches held their revival services. The "protracted meeting" was a week-long series of sermons and for many people it was the highlight of the summer. Relatives came from town to visit and attend the services where they would renew acquaintance with distant cousins as well as old friends, and enjoy wonderful food.

Farmers had a few days then after the wheat harvest and when corn had been "laid by" to take time away from the fields. Harvesting was weeks away and the opportunity to meet and talk with other farmers offered a welcome diversion.

A visiting minister would preach morning and afternoon throughout the week, a total of twelve sermons. He would be entertained in the home of a different family each night, be expected to eat dinner and a hearty breakfast next morning, and be back at church for an 11:00 o'clock service next day with energy undiminished. Revival speakers were men with phenomenal good health, endurance and enthusiasm. Furthermore, they had strong voices and could make themselves heard without the aid of public address systems. They thundered their messages above the sounds of wailing babies, whispers, and droning insects.

The morning service began at 11:00 A.M. and ended sometime around noon depending upon the length of the sermon and the number of extra hymns sung at its conclusion. When the benediction was said the hungry crowd surged toward the dinner tables spread in the yard.

Here ladies were busily unpacking boxes, hampers, and baskets of food, all prepared early that morning. The tables built for the occasion of rough lumber were arranged under the trees. Covered with an assortment of table cloths, they were loaded with food. Each family had a few feet of space for its dinner, then another family laid out its display of food. Piles of fried chicken, plates of ham, occasionally a dish of lamb and vegetables of every kind in season were spread in bountiful supply. The food was limited to what was raised on the farm, but it was provided in lavish quantity. For dessert there were pies and cakes and usually once during the week someone would bring a freezer of ice cream.

Ice itself was a special treat. If Mr. Walden brought a wagon with ice from his ice house, children crowded around for the chips as it was cracked and men came with glasses of tepid tea for a lump of ice to cool it as a special treat for a favored visitor. The freezer of ice cream heavily swathed in wrappings to prevent melting was dished out to everyone as long as it lasted.

The preachers were served first and bore away plates piled high with servings from as many family dinners as possible so as to slight no one. The exertions of the morning and the anticipated strenuous efforts of the afternoon required prodigious quantities of food apparently. Guests were urged to the tables next and home folks and children ate last.

Adolescents just becoming interested in the opposite sex found the dinner hour exciting. Couples with loaded plates found a shady spot, sat on the grass and ate hardly aware of what they were eating. Children were dragged forward to meet visiting relatives who would exclaim on "who he favored."

The afternoon service began when strains of the organ reached the ears of the people outside. Seats were soon filled and though no electric fans or air-conditioning alleviated the August heat, few failed to return to the crowded church.

At the end of the week there were usually a number of additions to the church and plans would be made for a baptismal service in a few weeks.

Baptisms were held on a Sunday afternoon during warm weather. There were no baptisteries in rural churches; the river, a creek or a pond convenient to the church provided sufficient water for the ceremony. A stream of surreys and buggies would travel slowly to the chosen location, usually a millpond. In a sense it was the perfect setting: the quiet waters ringed by trees, the slanting rays of the sun and the soft singing of the crowd left an indelible impression on the candidates for baptism.

The pastor waded into the waist-deep water; the boys and girls to be immersed, clad in white, followed hand in hand. Each rose, dripping from the water, and returned to the shore where a family member provided dry clothes. There was little formality, but the simplicity of the service was impressive.

The Baptist denomination was established in eastern Virginia just prior to the Revolution; the fiery preaching of early converts brought people into the church in large numbers. From the first, immersion was an important ritual. Mass baptisms are on record in the late 18th century and early 1800s. As new churches were established and became strong enough to function independently the customs of week-long revivals followed by open air baptisms became firmly entrenched.

The foregoing descriptions are typical of ceremonies held in all the Middle Peninsula Baptist Churches for over 150 years.

Baptisteries have eliminated the outdoor ceremonies today. Old churches not equipped with baptismal pools often use the facilities of a sister church. However, the natural setting recreating the first-century scene on the Jordan River still has great appeal.

Public Education Moved Slowly in Virginia

September means back to school for most people today, but in 1870 when Virginia passed the Education Act establishing a system of public education, many school sessions in rural areas were for only five months. Children were needed to harvest fall crops and to help with spring planting; school often began in late October and ended in March, depending on the growing season.

Schools were located to serve students living within a radius of four or five miles which was considered to be walking distance. There was no public transportation in most counties until after World War I when automobiles and trucks came into general use and roads improved. The first school buses were trucks with a covered body built over the chassis. These accommodations were greeted with great approval by rural families whose children either walked to school, rode a horse, or drove a buggy.

The typical one-room school stood in a location central to the community. It was a frame building about twenty by thirty feet with a hip roof and a heavy front door. Opposite the door was a platform about twelve inches high which extended across the width of the room. On it stood the teacher's desk and chair, and behind it was a blackboard. Sometimes a set of maps might be available. There were windows covered with heavy wooden shutters on each side. There was no lighting or plumbing.

The central feature of the room was a large cast iron stove which stood in a box of sand. A safety measure, it caught the live coals which often fell from the stove when it was being stoked. It was the teacher's duty to kindle the fire each winter morning, but older boys among the pupils split the kindling and brought in the wood.

Pupils' seats were handmade to accommodate four or five children. The top slanted so that anything put on it slid off into the pupil's lap or on the floor. All desks were the same size so that young children sat with their feet dangling inches from the floor. Such desks were not built for comfort.

Teachers took a qualifying examination and were issued a first or second grade certificate. Few had attended college. Young men would often take a teaching job for a year or so while preparing for some other vocation. Most teachers were unmarried women who gave up teaching if they married. Salaries in the first decade of this century were as low as $22.50 per month in some counties.

The teacher was expected to teach all subjects though the three R's (reading, writing, and arithmetic) formed the basic curriculum. Instruction was minimal. The teacher assigned some pages to be studied; the pupil returned to his seat until the teacher called him to "hear his lesson." She asked questions on the content and expected rote answers. Sums to be worked were often written on a slate. Joe Major, 95, of Saluda who attended Frog Pond Academy at Stormont recalls using a slate. "I'd spit on it and wipe it off with my sleeve after the teacher had corrected it," he said. Paper was scarce; slates lasted indefinitely.

At big recess the students ate a lunch brought in a tin bucket with a close-fitting top. It usually consisted of biscuits, meat, preserves, perhaps a sweet potato or an apple. After lunch the pupils enjoyed vigorous group games such as "prisoner's base," "run, sheep, run" or "annie over." There was no equipment and no organized recreation or physical education.

As the century advanced, the school year lengthened. Mrs. Emma Eastman Wrightson, 90, taught a one-room school at Samos in Middlesex County the session of 1921-22. By this time it was an eight-month term, but attendance was poor in the early fall and late spring, she said. Farmers who needed their children to help in the fields did not hesitate to keep them at home.

By the second decade of the century interest in public education was increasing. Many communities struggled to raise money to build schools which offered at least several years of high school work, but many one-and-two teacher units continued.

The division superintendent's annual report of Mathews County, session 1921-22, is representative of the surrounding rural counties. That year the following high schools were in operation: Cobbs Creek (seven teachers), Gwyns (five teachers), Peninsula (five), New Point (six), Lee-Jackson (seven). All had terms of nine months, but obviously only the schools with seven teachers provided four years of high school work. Some students attended private schools which offered college preparatory courses. Others, like Saluda residents, Mrs. Bettie Woodward James, Mrs. Louise Harwood Hedrick and Mrs. Eleanor Ball Kipps, finished high school at Fredericksburg Normal School (now Mary Washington College) which offered two years of high school and two years of college.

Separate elementary schools operating in Mathews the same year were Hallieford (two teachers), Cattail (two), North (one), Foster (two), Haven (three), Beaver Dam (one), Winter Harbor (three), Peary (one). Several of these had seven-month sessions.

The report also listed the following nine "colored" one-and-two teacher schools: Hudgins (two), North (two), Blakes (one), Haven (two), Glebe (one), Cardinal (two), Antioch (two), Wayland (one), Hamburg (one) all of which ran for seven months. There were no schools offering education beyond the seventh grade.

Nine years later (1930-31), the Superintendent's annual report showed considerable change: sessions were longer; certification showed more collegiate and normal professional certificates and fewer special certificates; salaries had not risen greatly, due to the Depression, no doubt, but the lowest salary listed was $55.00 per month. In 1921-22 approximately half the elementary teachers were receiving $55.00 monthly and fourteen received only $35.00.

These statistics refer only to one county but are representative of most rural counties on the Middle Peninsula in the same period.

After World War I, public transportation made possible the consolidation of high schools to offer a broader curriculum. Single-teacher units gradually disappeared and a modern system of education slowly developed.

Rappahannock Industrial Academy

On Route 17 near Dunnsville in Essex County stands a granite marker surrounded by a ring of boxwood. Nearby are two brick columns flanking a long, narrow lane leading between cultivated fields to a stand of tall trees; no buildings are in sight.

Passersby are intrigued by the marker and surmise that the imposing gateposts marked the entrance to an important building, but few know the real significance of the site.

Beyond these gateposts once stood the Rappahannock Industrial Academy, the first secondary school for the education of black boys and girls in the surrounding counties. Public education for blacks did not extend beyond seventh grade at that time.

Before the turn of the century the Southside Rappahannock Baptist Association, composed of thirty-eight churches, all but two from the counties of Essex, King and Queen and Middlesex, had initiated plans to "establish an institution stressing character and Christian education." The Site Committee eventually found a 159 acre farm and purchased it for $1,200.00. A part of this sum was contributed by the Women's Baptist District Missionary Convention which received twenty-five acres of the tract upon which it established a home for the aged.

The school opened in January 1902 in a farm house already on the property. However, by 1903 the cornerstone of the Towles Building, a three-story dormitory with accommodations for forty-five girls and two teachers, had been laid. It also contained the dining hall, chapel, and administrative offices. Later a second building provided rooms for thirty male students, two teachers, three classrooms, a library, and a laboratory.

During the Academy's operation, nine men and two women served as principals, some for only a year or two. However, in 1904, Professor W. Edward Robinson, a native of Middlesex County and a graduate of Howard University, assumed the post, a tenure that lasted for twenty-nine years. It was he who set the standards of the school and directed its growth and development to become an institution influencing the lives of many young people for almost half a century. It became an accredited high school in the late 1930s.

By 1948 the need for such a school had diminished. Public education with free transportation to high schools furnishing a broader curriculum was by then available and the school closed its doors after forty-six years.

From the beginning the Academy was funded by the Southside Rappahannock Baptist Association and the fees of the students. It could probably be described as a "no frills" institution which placed emphasis on academics first and foremost.

A schedule of the fees for the session of 1940-41 was as follows:

> Room and board for the first month $12.00
> Monthly room and board after first month $11.00
> Entrance Medical Examination fee $0.25
> Chemistry lab fee $1.50
> Monthly instrumental music fee (optional) $1.00

Records of the school dating from 1917 are now housed at Essex High School in Tappahannock. The property is still owned by the Association.

Miss Edwardine Robinson, 89, a retired teacher living at Locust Hill in Middlesex County, is the daughter of former principal, Professor W. E. Robinson. She grew up at the Academy and completed the three-year course of study to graduate in 1922; then she attended Hartshorn Memorial College in Richmond. This was a mission school which offered college preparatory work and from which she earned a diploma. She became a graduate of Virginia Union University in 1928 and returned to the Rappahannock Industrial Academy to teach for five years.

Miss Robinson's knowledge of the day-to-day operation of the school provides an intimate view of its activities. "The curriculum was college preparatory," she said. "Algebra and geometry, Latin, English and history comprised the course of study in the early years." Gradually science received increased emphasis. This basic instruction was comparable to that offered in other private schools and in the rural public schools in the first decades of this century. No credit was given for physical education, but there were some extra-curricular activities.

"The students kept their own rooms clean and groups were assigned on a rotating basis to clean the halls, stairways and public rooms," said Miss Robinson. "Since there was no central heating, the boys were required to keep the many stoves in wood during cold weather, a sizable job."

She continued:

> We usually had a cook who prepared the meals, but occasionally the older girls helped in the kitchen if we were short-handed.
>
> Classes began at 9:00 a.m., but before that we always had a devotional assembly. We sang several hymns and a faculty member or a student read from the Bible and led in prayer. We started the day on an inspirational and spiritual note. Papa always stressed the importance of faith and dependence on God and, of course, good character. He was long on that.
>
> The Dunbar Literary Society met every Friday night. If a student was on the program and failed to do his part, the penalty was that he had to perform on the following Tuesday at the Assembly.

She chuckled remembering the embarrassment of some of those reluctant participants. "There were no excuses, Papa was a strict disciplinarian."

After classes ended at 3:00 o'clock, the students had an opportunity for recreational activities. There was a basketball court, tennis and croquet, but baseball was the general favorite. There were even some match games with St. Clare Walker

High School in Middlesex and with another private school in Gloucester in the 1940s.

Emphasis was placed on choral music but without credit. There was also a debating team which provided training in public speaking and logical thinking.

The vision and wisdom of the men and women who recognized the need for a secondary school offering college preparatory work and who worked to construct and support it have been justified by the number of its successful graduates. The majority have gone on to college to become teachers, ministers, doctors, business men, and church and community leaders.

These men and women not only have served their communities, but also have provided role models for the rising generations.

The devotion of its graduates is evident in the loyal alumni association which holds frequent reunions. In 1982 this organization erected the marker on the site and held appropriate unveiling ceremonies. Serving also as a time capsule, it contains memorabilia of the academy to insure that its purpose and role are remembered in future years.

Rappahannock Industrial Academy Marker erected in 1982 by the Alumni Association.

Writing Instruments

The quill pen was the writing instrument of Colonial America. Thomas Jefferson drafted the Declaration of Independence on his famous lap desk using a quill. The Constitution of the United States was written and signed by the Founding Fathers with quill pens. They were used to draft wills, deeds, inventories and the legal papers of all kinds that are preserved in our local courthouses.

Writing is an ancient art, going back thousands of years. Writing materials were varied—stone, clay, papyrus and sheepskin. Likewise, different writing tools were employed: chisels for stone, the stylus for clay and a split reed for the papyrus of ancient Egypt. However, the feather or quill has been in use since Middle Ages. In fact, the word pen is derived from the Latin *penna* for feather.

Quills were taken from the wing feathers of a goose or other large bird. The end, sharpened to a fine point, produced a delicate script; a blunter point resulted in bolder lettering.

Letter writing, which was almost the only means of communication between friends and family, was done with a quill until the latter half of the 19th century. Both men and women carried on a lengthy correspondence, viewing it as an art to be good letter writers. Such letters have given us intimate glimpses into the daily life of the past. Now the telephone has virtually replaced the friendly letter. Business correspondence is the major form of modern letter writing.

Thomas Jefferson was a prolific writer. The body of his notes and correspondence is voluminous and the greater part was written with the quill. He was delighted with the polygraph, a two-pen writing device, invented by Charles Willson Peale, which Jefferson called the "finest invention of the modern age" and made use of in his later years.

The fact that documents of great age are still readable is due to the quality of the ink and paper on which they were written. Some ink faded more quickly than others due to its composition. Commercial inks were not always available and plantation owners sometimes made their own using strange mixtures. For instance, pokeberry juice produced a red ink and lampblack, of course, made black ink.

Foolscap, a high grade type of paper manufactured in the United States, was used for legal documents because of its durability. It measured thirteen by sixteen inches and carried the watermark of a fool's head and cap, hence its name.

Certain accessories were accompaniments to the quill pen. Ink stands or ink wells were produced in silver, pewter and porcelain in the 17th century and earlier. Later ones were made of glass in a variety of shapes.

Quill pens were eventually replaced by straight or stick pens which used a removable point called the nib. The steel points came in fine or medium points. Many pens were handsome with gold or mother of pearl shafts but most had wooden shafts and were utilitarian in purpose.

Dip pens made use of ink wells and other accessories such as pen cases and pen-wipers. The latter, often made by young ladies as small gifts, appeared in the form of tiny books, the leaves being scraps of flannel or other absorbent material on which the pen point would be wiped after use.

Blotters were a necessity for absorbing excess ink. Businessmen used them as give-aways, one side carrying the business name and advertising and the other heavy blotting paper. School children kept them in their books, ladies, with their writing materials, and bookkeepers always had a supply handy.

The dip pen was the pen possessed by every school child around the turn of the century. Learning to write with ink was a messy business for most of us who had started with a slate and pencil. Ink stained fingers, blots and even ink-stained clothing were the marks of school pupils. The Locker writing system required a copy book in which the pupil practiced circles and vertical lines over and over. Blots and blemishes on the writing paper were not well-received by the teachers.

School desks were furnished with a hole in the top for the necessary bottle of ink. Beside it was a deep groove to hold the pen to keep it from rolling down the slant top. These desks, as many readers may remember, were constructed with the back of one attached to the top of the one behind. The frame was cast iron and bolted to the floor. The open bottle of ink on the desk top offered an over-powering temptation to many mischievous boys to dip the long braids of the girl seated in front into the ink bottle. Such pranks were fairly routine.

Between 1870 and 1880, pen makers tried unsuccessfully to produce a pen with a self-contained ink reservoir. In 1884, Lewis Waterman, one of several American inventors, manufactured a pen that allowed ink to flow smoothly through a slit in the gold point. Made of vulcanite hard rubber, it had a reservoir filled with an eye-dropper.

By the 1890s, these improved pens were well-established. The Sears, Roebuck Catalog of 1897 carried two pages advertising fountain pens which it described as "the best made." The least expensive was offered at the special price of 65 cents; it had a pen point of fourteen carat solid gold. Others possessed pens of sixteen carat solid gold with holders of vulcanized rubber and sold for $1.25 for a plain model or up to $2.75 for a fancier model with the holder decorated in gold.

Solid gold, gold filled and sterling silver models were modestly priced. The highest priced model listed sold for $3.75.

By the early 1900s, Parker, Conklin, Shaeffer and Wahl Eversharp as well as Waterman were making pens. In 1905, Parker brought out a ribbon pen so named because it had a ring in the top of the cap and could be worn on a ribbon around the neck. The user unscrewed the cap and returned the pen to it after writing. Technical improvements soon resulted in the self-filling pens.

An early pen used a small lever on the outside of the barrel. When the lever was pulled open ink (or air) was forced out of the reservoir; when the pen was dipped in ink, the lever was released and suction filled the reservoir. This mechanism was soon replaced with an interior device that accomplished the same thing.

Handsome fountain pens appeared in color with gold or silver overlays as well as the plainer less expensive ones.

Fountain pens were status symbols when I was in high school and they retained their popularity through the 1960s when the convenient ballpoint pen made its appearance making ink unnecessary.

Today writing instruments are versatile, inexpensive tools meeting modern needs. We have the ballpoint, felt tip, metal tip and of course, specialty pens for drawing or calligraphy.

The fountain pen, once outmoded, is making a comeback. Pen makers are again producing expensive classic models for discriminating buyers. Strangely enough, the handsome earlier ones have become collector's items and often bring large sums.

Transportation/Travel

Sailing Vessels

Sailing vessels brought the first colonists to the New World and continued to transport its commodities for centuries. Gradually they developed into the great shipping fleets of two and three-masted vessels culminating in the four-masted ocean-going schooners, the clipper ships noted for their beauty and speed.

"Sailing vessels were an important part of life on the Chesapeake Bay from discovery until they were replaced by power vessels," said Lynn Perry, retired from the U.S. Navy and now living in Urbanna. He recalled:

> The beauty of these vessels under sail was wonderful. As a small boy growing up in West Point, Virginia, I became familiar with many of them when they anchored in the York River before sailing up the Mattaponi or the Pamunkey. I knew the captains and often went aboard.
>
> I was fascinated by the rigging, the skill and seamanship required to sail them and the details of life on board. With my box camera I took pictures of many of them. Learning about them became a life-time hobby.

By the first decades of this century the steamboat had taken over passenger service and handled some freight, but sailing craft still made up much of the commercial traffic in local waters. Heavy cargoes such as lumber, grain, and coal, were hauled by schooners, many captained by local men.

In the 1920s the thriving lumber industry of King and Queen County shipped quantities of rough lumber to Northern markets by way of the Mattaponi River. Vessels could go up-river as far as Ayletts, thirty-three miles above West Point, taking on cargo at various landings.

The late W. S. Beane of King and Queen Court House, whose father owned two lumber mills, recalled the excitement and activity which surrounded the arrival of the *Blackbird*, the *L. E. Williams*, or the *John R. P. Moore* at Melrose or King and Queen C. H. Landing. Captains of these vessels, whom Beane recalled were Capt. Lee and Captain John Insley. Such vessels could carry approximately 125,000 to 150,000 board feet of lumber in their holds and on deck. They would arrive riding high in the water, he said, to depart heavily loaded making their way slowly and majestically down river to enter the York and proceed up the Chesapeake Bay to Baltimore.

Sailing vessels came up the Piankatank as far as Freeport, about twenty-five miles from its mouth. Stands of cypress timber seldom found this far north grew in great abundance along the Dragon, the name given to the upper length of this stream. Logs and cut timber were brought down on barges to be loaded at Freeport. Vessels preparing for long voyages were said to have filled their water barrels from the Dragon because the water had medicinal value and kept better than spring water. Trees growing along the banks gave the water a characteristic brown stain from the tannic acid found in the bark which gave it healthful properties.

Schooner traffic in local waters continued until the late 1930s. A familiar sight on the Rappahannock River was the *Kate H. Tilghman*, built in 1881 in Maryland. In her last years she was owned and operated by Capt. R. O. Smith, Sr., of Urbanna; W. S. Cannon of Urbanna was also master at one time. She carried freight such as lumber, grain and watermelons. The *Tilghman* was abandoned in Urbanna Creek in 1944 where a part of her hull is still visible at low tide.

Gracie Mae was built in 1909 for Capt. Raymond Bristow of Dutton, Virginia, and was used to freight cargoes of grain and lumber. After she was converted to power and renamed the *Ruth Conway*, two local men served aboard her. Willie Sears of Harcum was mate and Leonard Turner of King and Queen was engineer.

Another schooner which saw service in local waters was the *W. J. Mathews* owned and operated for a time by the W. J. Marshall Oyster Co. of West Point. She was converted to power in 1934; she was listed as "abandoned" in 1969 in *Merchant Vessels of the United States*.

One of the last schooners to operate in the Piankatank was the *Columbia, F. C.*, acquired by Capt. Tom Henry Ruark in 1946. She remained in use here only two years for Capt. Ruark sold her to a Cuban firm in 1948.

One of the best accounts of life aboard a schooner can be found in *Harvesting the Chesapeake, Tools and Traditions* by Larry S. Chowning (Tidewater Publishers, Centreville, Md., 1990). The chapter entitled "Schooner Captain" details the reminiscences of Capt. Hugh Norris of Deltaville, now nearing 95, who worked as mate and as captain on some half dozen schooners.

"The *Maggie* was one of my favorites," he said. "She was the fastest of all the boats I worked aboard. Capt. Phil Ruark was her skipper and she carried a three-man crew on the boat."

Another of his favorites was the Joseph T. Brennan:

> Prettiest little boat you've ever seen. She wasn't big enough to run lumber on her. We ran potatoes and watermelons in spring and summer and the captain would buy oysters in the winter and haul them to Crisfield (Maryland).
>
> I hated to see the sailboats go, but all good things do come to an end, you know,

said Norris with a resigned shake of his head.

When the pageant of the sailing vessels ended, a colorful part of our past disappeared.

Schooner **Charles G. Joyce** *built in 1882. This vessel freighted lumber for J. H. Coulbourn of King and Queen County. During this period Capt. B. F. Collier was master and Willie Sears was mate. Both men were from Gloucester County. Lynn Perry of Middlesex County also sailed in the* Joyce. *Photo courtesy of Lynn Perry.*

The Gwynn's Island Bridge, built in 1939, has a swivel center span which opens for passage of boats across Milford Haven. It replaced a small powered ferry.

Ferries

If you had lived on Gwynn's Island a hundred years ago and wanted to go to Mathews Court House, you would have taken the ferry, paying twenty-five cents round trip for your horse and buggy.

Only a few years earlier the trip would have been even more difficult. You would have rowed your skiff across the "narrows" of Milford Haven with your horse swimming behind.

On the mainland you would have hitched the horse to a buggy kept there for your use and driven to the court house. Returning, you would have reversed the procedure to complete a time-consuming trip.

The Gwynn's Island ferry began operations in 1884 through the efforts of some local men who formed a stock company to provide the service. This hand-powered cable ferry was replaced by a barge propelled by a motor boat lashed alongside.

Later still that arrangement was replaced by a small powered ferry. In 1939, ferry service ended with the building of the present steel bridge with its swivel center span.

Ferry service was the normal way of crossing waterways from the early 17th century until well into the 20th century. Colonists in Tidewater, with its maze of streams, coves, creek and inlets, found boats a necessity.

Boat owners furnished transportation across rivers as a convenience for neighbors and travelers, but as settlements increased, a demand for more reliable transportation within the colony led to the establishment of public ferries.

The General Court in 1640 granted a patent to Henry Hawley to keep a ferry "at the mouth of Hampton Roads in

Kecoughtan" with the provision that he charge no more than a penny for the service. This was the first public ferry in Virginia.

In 1664 the Colonial Council ordered a ferry to cross the Piankatank at a location that became known as Turk's Ferry. This crossing, which connected Middlesex and Gloucester counties for the first time, remained in use until about 1915.

In 1792, following the American Revolution, the General Assembly passed legislation that ferries be kept constantly in operation at designated places. The list included fourteen locations on the James below Richmond, fourteen on the York below West Point, and six on the Rappahannock below Tappahannock.

Rates for ferriage were fixed by the assembly. Ferrymen, in recognition of the importance of their services, were exempt from musters, road-building and other duties.

An important link between Gloucester County and the lower peninsula was maintained by the ferry running from Gloucester Point to Yorktown. The George P. Coleman Memorial Bridge now provides this link.

Middlesex and Lancaster were connected by the Grey's Point Ferry until 1957, when the Robert O. Norris Bridge spanning the Rappahannock was built.

Beginning in 1911, Twigg's Ferry crossed the Piankatank from Mathews to Middlesex. It provided 24-hour service until 1953, when the half-mile long steel and concrete bridge in use today was opened.

Chain Ferry, a cable ferry, crossed the Mattaponi linking King and Queen County with West Point from a point a mile or so above the present bridge. This ferry is perpetuated in the name of a secondary road, Chain Ferry Road, which skirts the river on the King and Queen side.

River Highways and Rolling Roads

The roads "were hopeless seas of mud with archipelagoes of stumps" wrote a traveler in Virginia during the American Revolution.

How could such deplorable conditions have existed over 150 years after colonizations? One reason was that the need for good roads for military use had not been recognized; Indian war parties kept to the woods. There were other contributing factors, however.

Rivers were the first highways for the colonists. Exploration in the New World was done along the waterways. Settlers took up land first along the James, the York, the Rappahannock, and their tributaries moving inland gradually. After mid-seventeenth century great plantations were being established with imposing mansions such as Westover, Carter's Grove, and Rosegill, each built facing the river. Wharves and piers extended into the water where canoes, barges, and pinnaces were tied ready for use. Members of wealthy families attended weddings and funerals by boat. Ralph Wormeley of Rosegill sailed up the Rappahannock to visit his friend Gawin Corbin at Buckingham some ten miles away because travel by boat was faster and more comfortable than by horseback.

For settlers living inland travel overland was apt to be on foot or on horseback. Indian paths were narrow but wide enough to accommodate pedestrians or riders. If a wife accompanied her husband, she perched behind him on a pillion as they traveled to church, to court, or to visit a neighbor.

The first highway law in the New World was passed by the Virginia Assembly. It required highways to be "layd out at convenient places . . . as parishioners shall agree." Each county court was authorized to see that roads were constructed to the churches and to the court house. The appointed overseer of highways had the power to call upon "all males sixteen years and up, slave or free," to give several days of free labor annually on the roads. Lacking expertise or enthusiasm, such a labor force did not produce good roads.

Consequently, it was not until the development of the tobacco industry that roads became really important. Getting the tobacco crop to authorized tobacco ports on the various rivers required overland transportation of sorts. Tobacco had to be inspected before it could be shipped to England; thus growers could no longer ship from private wharves in their own vessels although some planters sent their tobacco crop to port by river traffic.

The cured tobacco leaves were packed in huge casks or barrels weighing up to a 1000 pounds; they could be rolled along the ground propelled by a man or hauled by oxen. Such traffic formed a beaten path which took the easiest route across fields, around trees, up hills at the gentlest slope, and across streams at fording places or make-shift bridges. Swampy ground was sometimes covered by laying poles close together across the muddy track and covering them with a thin layer of earth, known as "corduroy roads;" they were passable but rough. Vestiges of these rolling roads can still be seen in places. One, known as Prettyman's Rolling Road in colonial times, leads to Urbanna Creek, a designated tobacco port, between twenty-foot banks, centuries of traffic having worn the road to its present level.

At the end of the Revolution, the fledgling government had many pressing problems—one of them the building and maintaining of an adequate transportation system.

Ordinaries, Taverns and Inns

George Chowning, who kept an ordinary in 1735 in the town of Urbanna, was granted a license with the stipulations that he provide "good wholesome and cleanly Lodging and Diet for Travelers and Stableage and Provender for their horses . . . and shall not permit any unlawful gaming . . . nor on the Sabbath Day suffer any person to tipple or drink anymore than necessary." Chowning and other keepers of ordinaries were men of prominence in the community whose establishments were regulated by the local government.

The 17th century ordinaries came into existence to meet a specific need. Travel was slow and travelers were forced to spend the night on the road if a journey covered more than a few miles. An enterprising settler who lived on a river and owned a log canoe, for instance, might offer ferry service for a few pence. He would also provide a bed and meal in his home if it were needed. The accommodations would be crude but would at least give shelter and protection to someone on the road.

The terms ordinary and tavern were used interchangeably in 17th and 18th century Virginia. Webster's Unabridged Dictionary defines an ordinary as an eating place in which regular meals are served at a fixed price; also a place often used for gambling.

Without regulation at first, ordinaries charged whatever the keeper thought the traveler could pay. Due to the great price range and the increasing number, the General Assembly in 1639 passed legislation limiting rates to "12 pence for a meal or a gallon of beer." Enforcement was lax, however, and excessive rates remained common.

Keepers of ordinaries were often accused of over-charging, adulterating the liquor served, and of operating places, "the site of tumults and riots." Nevertheless, taverns increased to the point that by 1688 the Assembly limited the number to one or two to a county. Recreation then included gaming. cockfighting and horse-racing. Arguments often broke out which resulted in fist-fighting, eye-gouging and even dueling.

An ordinary or tavern always was located near the county seat; courthouses then as now were the center of business transactions. Court often lasted several days and judges, lawyers, and litigants needed lodging. They also grew up along turnpikes as well as near ferries and in villages and hamlets.

The quality of accommodations varied greatly. Raleigh Tavern in Williamsburg provided sumptuous meals, a well-stocked bar, and clean comfortable beds. At the other extreme, in backwoods country the service might be no more than a bed already occupied by another traveler or even two! The meal might be as simple as hoecake, so named because originally it was cooked on the blade of a hoe in the coals of a fire. If the traveler was lucky, he could find coffee or whiskey to wash down the unpalatable fare. Harrowing accounts of conditions in frontier lodgings appear in letters and diaries of many colonial travelers.

Taverns and ordinaries served as social centers, gathering-places where men (never any women) could meet to drink a glass of whiskey or beer and exchange news. Newspapers were few and circulation was poor so that such places met a vital need for communication. In more recent times the country store with its pot-bellied stove and circle of men swapping yarns met the same need.

Today the name ordinary survives in a few places. Sewall's Ordinary near Gloucester Point is an example. A pre-Revolutionary building, it was first used as an ordinary, then a private home, and later a restaurant. George Washington is said to have stayed there on his trips to Williamsburg from his Westmoreland County home. Nearby was a race track where he may have raced his own horses or have been a spectator.

Abingdon Glebe, another historic Gloucester property, is believed to have been used as an ordinary in the early 1800s when, after the Disestablishment of the Episcopal Church, it had been county property. It has been privately owned for many years.

At King and Queen Court House The Tavern, the only building to escape burning by Federal troops in 1864, is now used as an office building.

In Urbanna the building where George Chowning served his clients in 1735 is still known as The Old Tavern and the story still persists that Patrick Henry delivered one of his fiery speeches from its front steps.

The Tavern at King and Queen Court House.

Bridges Over the Dragon

Dragon Swamp originates in Essex County not far from the King and Queen County line. It writhes its way eastward to join Dragon Run which has its headwaters in the vicinity of Millers Tavern. The two streams unite to form the unique body of water known as the Dragon. Its meandering course eastward forms the boundary between King and Queen and Essex Counties along its upper length and Gloucester and Middlesex Counties lower down. As it widens, it eventually becomes a tidal stream, the Piankatank.

As colonization advanced inland in the seventeenth century there were settlements along both sides of the stream which necessitated methods of crossing. Communication between plantations and settlements was vital in colonial days. No doubt the first crossings were by boat. The Indian dugout canoe, which Captain John Smith made use of on many occasions, was quickly adapted for use by the early settlers until boats of a more conventional type were constructed. However, the need for a bridge was soon evident.

The first bridge was built by order of the Colonial Council in 1667. It reads:

> Where as there is an order for making a bridge on the Dragon Swamp, the north side of which is in Lancaster County (now Middlesex) and the other side where the bridge will come uncertain whether in Gloucester or New Kent, it is proposed that all three counties contribute to the making of the bridge.

It will be remembered that King and Queen County was a part of New Kent until 1691 when King and Queen became a separate entity.

Keeping up bridges in colonial times appears to have been somewhat of a problem as the following incident reveals. In 1672 the General Court of Virginia records that an arrogant Virginia gentleman who had behaved in a "contemptious [*sic*] manner" to the county commissioners was ordered to apologize publicly and to pay 400 pounds of tobacco toward building and "mending the bridge over the great swamp betwixt Gloucester and Middlesex." This solution benefited the locality at least and, it is hoped, taught the gentleman to be more careful in venting his ire in the future.

Bird's Bridge on Rt. 604 connecting Essex County and King and Queen between Center Cross and Hollow Chestnut (now Ino) may have been the second bridge over the Dragon. Colonial records contain a petition from the Bird family presented in 1744 for a public road to connect bridges and a causeway which they had "privately built over the Dragon Swamp very convenient for themselves and the public to pass to and from the Rappahannock and the Mattaponi Rivers."

This appeal was probably made by Robert Armistead Bird, grandson of Robert Bird, who had patented land in 1691 "in the forks of a branch that runneth into Exoll's branch" (a tributary of the Dragon). By early eighteenth century the Bird property had increased to nearly 2000 acres extending to the bridge now bearing this name and beyond. It is probable, therefore, that the first crossing had been built for private use long before the appeal for a public road. The family continued to hold property in this area into the nineteenth century. One of the oldest homes in the county known as the Bird Place still stands only a mile or two from the bridge which perpetuates the family name.

Wares Bridge on Rt. 602 was probably built shortly before the Revolution. The name may have derived from the local name for Lower King and Queen Church, which was constituted in 1772 and became known as Wares from the name of the first pastor, Robert Ware. Glebe Landing, another Baptist congregation, had been formed in upper Middlesex also in 1772 and there was frequent communication between the two groups. The bridge made passage easy for residents on both sides of the Dragon.

The fact that the name of the bridge does not appear on the Peter Jefferson-Joshua Frye Map of 1755 lends credence to the belief that this bridge was built later. Only two crossings appear on the map: the 1667 bridge and the one at Bestland near the county line in Essex. This bridge crosses a tributary before the confluence of the two branches forms Dragon Run.

Another bridge was built in the 1830s and is still referred to as New Dragon Bridge to distinguish it from the first which appeared on some maps as Old Dragon Bridge. It crosses the Dragon on Route 603 which leads to the community of Mascot.

The narrow Dragon widens quite suddenly a few miles below Saluda to become the Piankatank River. Here the marsh extends into the water to offer a shallow footing used by the Indians as a crossing. This became the site of the earliest crossing of the stream, a ferry which remained in use until the early 1900's.

Edward Nauman, who owned and operated this ferry, designed and built the last of the Dragon bridges. Considered to be something of a mechanical genius, he constructed a bridge with a very high central section with piling far enough apart for scows (barges) to pass between thus eliminating the need for a draw. This was a private toll bridge; toll was quite small, perhaps fifty cents for a vehicle and five cents for a pedestrian, according to local legend.

Barges went upstream to load with lumber and bring it down to be loaded on larger vessels for shipment to northern markets.

The bridge was demolished when a barge crashed into it and it was never rebuilt.

All traffic across the stream at this point ended in the 1920s.

Other means of crossing the Dragon must have been used by landowners living at a distance from the established bridges before modern means of transportation. Slaves probably waded or poled a flat-bottom boat across when occasion demanded. It also may have been possible to ford it on horseback in shallow places.

Tributaries of the Dragon are numerous. Exol, perhaps the largest of these, has been bridged at several places, such as Motleys Mill near Carlton Store and another between Ino and Dragonville close to the point where the stream joins the Dragon.

My Lady's Swamp is a tributary of the Piankatank River. An amusing story exists regarding its whimsical name and that of the bridge which crosses it on Route 629. In Colonial days, so the story goes, Madame Grymes, who lived at Grymesby on the river wished to visit Rosegill. Her husband sent the lady in her sedan chair borne by four slaves on the outing. On the return trip the bearers stumbled, dropped the chair in the water, and madame's feet got wet. Her husband promptly ordered a bridge to be built across the swamp to avoid future accidents. The bridge and swamp both go by the name My Lady's today.

Today a good system of public roads makes travel over these bridges easy and convenient.

The first crossing of the Dragon at this place was made by the Bird family for their private use. The sign uses an alternate spelling.

The Steamboat Era

The steamboat era is remembered fondly by many people who enjoyed delightful trips in the luxurious splendor of a favorite steamer and who still regret the ending of this colorful chapter in early twentieth century life.

Elizabeth Harrow, a resident of Saluda who grew up in Deltaville, recalled many trips to Baltimore with her sisters to visit their grandparents. She remembered:

> Father would put us on the boat at Jackson Creek Wharf. He knew the captain of the *Middlesex*, one of the steamboats we often took, and he'd ask him to look out for us. When it was bedtime, the captain would send a chambermaid to put us to bed and see that we were all right. I'd always take the upper berth; my sister Marian didn't like to sleep there, but I thought it was fun.
>
> We'd get to Baltimore about nine o'clock after a big breakfast. They served the best food on those boats.

William F. Grinels of Wake also recalls traveling to Baltimore with his parents and his brother. "Jim and I loved those big bathtubs with the sloping end and made good use of them," he smiled in recollection.

"We'd get on at North End Wharf where my grandparents lived. The fare for my parents was around $8.00 round trip. Children went for half-price. Breakfast and dinner (lunch) was 75 cents a piece and supper was $1.00 each."

The run from Baltimore to Fredericksburg provided transportation for young people going to school in Fredericksburg, Richmond and even Williamsburg. In the first quarter of this century Fredericksburg Normal School offered two years of high school work as well as two years of college. Among the young ladies from Saluda who attended school there were Bettie Woodward James and Louise Harwood Hedrick. Mrs. Hedrick recalled:

> We had some hilarious times on the trips up river. Criss-crossing the river from wharves on the Southside to wharves on the Northern Neck side, the boat picked up students at each stop. Boys going to William and Mary or Richmond College would get the train in Fredericksburg to Richmond or on to Williamsburg. That was before we had the bridge at Tappahannock and automobiles were few anyway.

Bettie James remembered:

> Coming home was different. We'd take the boat about 2:00 p.m. and get as far as Leedstown, where it anchored until about 3:30 a.m. Then it would start downriver, and we might get to Urbanna by 5:00 if we had a good wind and tide.
>
> We'd have a stateroom and go to bed about midnight sometimes. If it was a moonlight night we'd stay on deck dancing and singing and having a wonderful time.

Mrs. Hedrick recalled an occasion when the students were coming home for Christmas and the ice closed in and the boat was stuck for several days.

"The captain said we were pests; we made too much noise with our dancing and singing and in addition we ate up all his Christmas candy," said Mrs. Hedrick.

Mrs. James recalled the slow passage up river:

> The boat would be so close to shore in places you could almost touch the trees growing on the bank. In other places the channel was a long ways from shore. Bowler's Wharf (Essex County) had a pier almost a mile long.

The first steamship to sail the Chesapeake Bay was the *Chesapeake* constructed in Baltimore in 1813. Crude by later standards, it was propelled by side-wheels ten feet in diameter. It provided service for first-class passengers only and certainly offered more comfortable and reliable transportation than the sailing packets available then. Steamboat traffic continued to increase steadily along the rivers flowing into the Bay.

The first steamboat on the Rappahannock River was the *Patuxent* which made an experimental run to Fredericksburg in 1828. By 1830 the *Rappahannock* was making regular runs in the river. Among steamboats operating before the Civil War were the *Virginia* and the *William Seldon*, both of which burned in 1862.

The Piankatank River did not have steamboat service until 1873 when the Maryland Steamboat Company opened a route with the *Massachusetts* which made only two trips weekly. The *Enoch Pratt, Ida,* and *Avalon* also made trips on this river in the 1880s.

Runs were developed on the Mattaponi and Pamunkey Rivers which flow together at West Point to form the York River, all before the Civil War. Although normal river traffic was disrupted during the war, it resumed quickly at the conclusion of hostilities.

In the early decades of this century travel by boat to Baltimore, Norfolk and Fredericksburg was pleasant, convenient, comfortable and inexpensive. Regular schedules were operating on all local rivers providing passenger service and freight handling.

The steamer *Middlesex*, a side-wheeler built in 1902, was referred to as "the nattiest American side-wheeler." In 1919 she was making trips three times a week up the Rappahannock River to Fredericksburg.

In 1908 the *Mobjack*, a side-wheeler operated by the Old Dominion Steamship Company, was making daily trips from Norfolk to Mobjack Bay to pick up cargoes and passengers. She stopped at East River wharves daily, at North and Severn River wharves three times a week and at wharves on the Ware River on the alternate days. She handled fish, crabs, clams, potatoes and other vegetables in summer; in winter oysters were shipped as well as other cargo.

An article appearing in *History and Progress, Mathews County, Va.* (1982) quotes Robert Morton Sigman, who was purser on the *Mobjack*. He described the services the ship provided for the counties of Gloucester and Mathews. In summer the ship brought ice from Old Point and sold it at wharves where it stopped. It was the only way the area could get manufactured ice at that time.

A roll call of steamboats plying the waters of the Chesapeake tributaries would reveal names of counties: *Lancaster, Essex, Middlesex, Westmoreland;* names of bodies of water: the *Piankatank,* the *Rappahannock,* the *Mobjack;* names of cities: the *Norfolk, Baltimore, Newport News* and, of course, the names of many people.

Some of these steamboats were noted for their luxurious interiors. The *Lancaster,* for instance, had a saloon which could seat forty or fifty people, a dining room serving excellent meals, comfortable staterooms, and even a bridal suite with a double bed.

The steamboat era began to decline after World War II, one reason being faster and cheaper overland transportation, which was increasing with the development of good roads and the construction of bridges over many waterways.

The Talbot *entering Urbanna Creek. Photo courtesy of Buddy Davis.*

Top Buggies and Surreys

The top buggy was the preferred vehicle for country people during the latter part of the 19th century and the first quarter of the 20th. Prior to the Civil War well-to-do families possessed a carriage for travel to and from church and for social visits. Business travel might be by horseback and the work vehicle was the wagon. After the war impoverished gentlemen declined to use the carriage which needed a driver who cared for the horses as well. Buggies were less expensive and more practical. The buggy was lighter in construction, could travel faster, required one horse rather than two or even four, and could travel the bad roads with less difficulty. For family use there was the surrey.

A buggy could accommodate two adults (if they were not very heavy) and a child squeezed between them. A single occupant had it a little better. Drummers, the traveling salesman of the era, used the buggy loading the boot, foot and seat with their samples. They stopped at hotels or taverns where the horses were stabled and fed and the buggy greased if necessary for the next day's travel.

The 1902 Sears, Roebuck Catalogue offered a number of buggies for sale ranging in price from $34.95, the cheapest, to $54.90 for the Acme Royal Top Buggy, the most expensive.

The catalogue gave highly descriptive details for each one. The "wonder buggy" ($34.95) had a leather top, side curtains of black enameled drill, upholstered seat, wheels made of reinforced hickory stock, steel tires, high-grade springs and strong axles. The Acme Royal, it claimed, was made of better materials with even better workmanship and was guaranteed for one year. Country people read the glowing advertisements and ordered their vehicles shipped by freight or express. Sears was well represented in our community.

My earliest memories are of riding in a buggy. Someone hitched Nellie to take the wash to the laundress, to go to the post office three miles away, or for longer trips to the blacksmith's shop, to the doctor, or to visit. I was usually occupying a limited space in the seat between my mother and my aunt, not really comfortable but unaware of it because I was intrigued by the whip in the whip socket and the spatter board. This amenity protected the occupants, from sand and dust kicked up by the horse's hooves and from splashes of mud when a mud puddle appeared in the road. The buggy whip was seldom used except to "touch up" Nellie to a trot along level stretches of the road. Going up a hill made the horse pull harder and going down caused the buggy to roll toward the horse so his tail was almost in the buggy, kept out by the spatter board.

I was a very proud person when I was allowed to drive alone to the store or go on some errand. In high school I occasionally drove to school and found it pleasing to have one of the boys tie the horse for me and feed him from the bunch of fodder tied on the back of the buggy.

Travel by buggy was not always enjoyable. In winter the occupants got the full force of the wind and so had to wear heavy clothing: caps, scarves, mittens and extra socks; hot bricks in the foot alleviated the discomforts of cold feet, to some extent. In summer it was necessary to wear a duster (a light, loose, cotton coat worn over suit or dress) if one wanted to arrive with a presentable appearance. In rainy weather the removable curtains could be snapped in place but these obstructed viewing, and were troublesome to put on, so often it seemed not worth the trouble.

Short trips involved six to ten miles. A trip to Urbanna was a long trip of twenty miles and took all day. We carried feed for the horse (hay or fodder) tied over the boot in the back. When we crossed a stream the horse would stop to drink if it was thirsty.

There was not much storage in a buggy. Feet took up most of the floor space, but there was the "boot" back of the seat, a space eight or ten inches deep with a hinged cover in which something could be carried. When we visited relatives in Urbanna there were usually products from the farm in the boot. Buggies transported people; wagons transported loads.

The buggy was a fine thing for courting. A young man groomed his buggy as carefully as today's youth wash and shine the automobile. He cleaned mud from the wheels until the spokes were bright and shining, the shafts were rubbed and cleaned. The horse received special attention also. The horse's harness was oiled and polished, and his bridle sometimes sported a red tassel. The horse's mane was combed, its tail was washed and braided, and its coat was combed and shining. Such a stylish horse and buggy caused heads to turn. Any girl would be flattered to ride in it.

The surrey was a two-seat conveyance. It could seat two adults front and back, but it often was pushed to carry more. It required two horses to pull it. The surrey was equipped with springs so the ride was not too rough; however, there was a disagreeable side. The canopy with its jaunty fringe gave a carnival air to the ride, but it offered scant protection from sun, wind or rain. Dust kicked up by the horses' hooves and the wheels settled on driver and occupants alike. It was not a vehicle for all seasons. The ride to church in winter was punishing. Bundled up in coats, scarves, and lap robes, we arrived half frozen to cluster around the enormous heaters until we thawed out.

There were two other horse-drawn vehicles which I remember: the topless or open buggy and the road cart. The road cart had two wheels and a single seat; it was light and the rider could make good time in it, but it offered no protection at all. In 1897 Sears offered a road cart for $17.00. Men liked them for errands but no lady used a road cart.

Such vehicles served the rural population until automobiles began to appear. Even then, country people remained loyal to the horse and buggy for some time. The automobile was the rich man's toy at first; it was unsuited to country roads and country needs.

In 1904 Oldsmobiles sold for $650 each and some 5000 were purchased. In 1908 Henry Ford introduced the Model-T and its low price made it attractive to a larger number of buyers. Country people living along primary roads bought before farmers who had only dirt roads to travel.

After World War I in the 1920s, improved roads made automobile travel more practical, but getting stuck on an unpaved road was far from unusual. With wheels spinning and mud flying, the car would not move, and the hapless travelers had to push it, put branches under the wheel to gain traction, and sometimes even find a farmer with a team of mules to pull the car out. The buggy owner who had no problem with the narrow buggy wheels and horse power to get him where he was going laughed at the "horseless carriage." Eventually he too succumbed to the appeal of the automobile with its comfortable seats, its curtains for protection against the elements and its speed over good roads. The buggy house ceased to house the buggy and became the garage for the new Ford instead. Gradually the "horse-and-buggy era" came to an end.

Local History

Man of Mystery

History is filled with the difficulties encountered by the first English colonists in Virginia. Hostility between the Native Americans and the Europeans began long before the settlement at Jamestown. Settlers found the Powhatan Indians (a term encompassing a number of tribes in Tidewater) by turns friendly and hostile, but Opechancanough, brother and successor to Chief Powhatan, bore an unmitigated hatred of all Europeans. It was he who master-minded and executed the devastating massacres of 1622 and 1644.

Was there a reason, born perhaps of some personal experience, which accounted for his long and unyielding antagonism?

The answer to this question may be found in an intriguing story of an Indian youth, kidnapped by a Spanish sailing vessel, who eventually was returned to his homeland. Scholars are not in agreement as to the identity of this man who may have become a powerful figure after his return, but there are tantalizing speculations.

During the 16th century Spanish ships dominated the Caribbean and even sailed the Atlantic as far north as Canada. Ships' logs provide fascinating accounts of their encounters with the "savages." On one voyage a Spanish commander picked up a likely Indian boy and took him with him to Mexico. Such kidnappings were not unusual. Both Spanish and English ships employed the practice; if the youth picked up the language he could be useful on other voyages as an interpreter.

This young boy was intelligent and quickly learned to speak Spanish. He was taken to Spain where he took the name of his sponsor, Don Luis de Velasco, converted to Christianity, and appeared to embrace the Spanish culture as well. Eventually he was returned to Havana where he encouraged an attempt to found a Jesuit mission in what is now Tidewater Virginia.

The first attempt was unsuccessful, but in 1570 in the second attempt a Spanish ship brought eight Jesuit missionaries, a novice named Alonso de Lara and Don Luis to a location on the James River. For some unknown reason the group soon moved to a place on the York River inhabited by the Chiskiaks, a tribe not related to the Don.

Although Don Luis appeared to be a Spanish nobleman, wearing Spanish garb, his tribal loyalty was still strong. By the end of two days he left the mission and returned to his relatives on the James. It is possible that the founding of the mission had been a clever ruse he had planned to accomplish his return to his own people.

The missionaries were soon in need of supplies. They had expected help from their Indian friend in securing food and in converting his tribesman. They sent repeated appeals to Don Luis to return but he ignored them. At last in desperate straits, three of the number visited him, demanding his return but with no success. They were killed soon after they started back.

A few days later Don Luis and a party of warriors arrived at the mission, and on the pretext of helping to fell trees, killed the remaining five priests with their own axes. They spared Alonso against the advice of the Don who knew that a Spanish ship would come to retaliate.

In time a relief ship came and found the mission empty. A party of warriors attacked the sailors and in the encounter one was taken captive; then the ship returned to Cuba. This man told them that Alonso was still alive, so in 1572 a ship was sent to rescue him.

The commander of the rescue ship was met by a band of hostile Indians some of which he captured and held hostage in an attempt to secure Alonso's release. He sent one of the captives to Don Luis ordering him to appear or he would kill the remaining captives in his place. The order was ignored, and the commander carried out his threat killing several captives and releasing the others. Alonso, who had been taken to a different location, was returned later to the rescue ship and eventually to his homeland where he recounted these events.

Don Luis disappears from the pages of history at this point, but speculations about his Indian identity remain. What tribal name did he bear? Did he assume a position of leadership in the tribe? Why did he distrust and hate the Europeans? Did he perhaps recognize the clash of cultures and foresee the destruction of the way of life of his people?

To assume that Don Luis and Opechancanough were one and the same gives a plausible explanation for his role in 17th century Virginia history. Some scholars have accepted the story as fact although it cannot be proved for the Indians left no written records. Other historians feel that the pieces of the puzzle do not fit exactly and reject the story. Nevertheless, the possibility is a fascinating one to students of history.

The Colonial Militia

The military system of our nation, built over the past two centuries to protect us against dangers within or without, represents a tremendous aggregation of manpower, materiel, and money. From what small beginnings did this mighty machine develop?

When the first Englishmen were establishing themselves as the Virginia Colony, they were faced with tremendous and constant dangers: hostile Indians, wild animals, rebellions, and at a later time, slave insurrections. What military defenses did the colonial government establish for the settlers' protection in those perilous times?

Few military records for the first century exist, but there was a colonial militia, a loose organization designed to bring colonists together for common defense in times of danger. History makes frequent mention of clashes where the settlers were armed and fought.

Middlesex County Museum has on display the muster roll of a local troop. Written on yellowing paper, brittle with age, the document begins: "The Appearance of the Lower Troop of Middlesex County on the 26th day of September 1730 at their place of Exercise."

Headed by the names of Capt. Blackburn and Lt. James Daniel, the list contains thirty-nine names, many of them still familiar ones in the county today; some of them are: Bristow, Clarke, Davis, Jones, Smith, Weston, and Wood.

Robert Beverley of Beverley Park in King and Queen County, is the author of the first comprehensive history of the Virginia Colony. Published in 1705 in England under the title *A History of the Present State of Virginia*, the book covers the early history and such topics as the natural history, Indians, the clergy, the courts, the militia, and others.

Every freeman from sixteen to sixty, he wrote, was listed in the militia. The governor of the colony was Lieutenant-General and appointed the major officers of each county unit which was subdivided into troops or companies. An annual general muster was required but troop musters were held three or four times a year, usually on holidays: Christmas, Easter, and Whitsuntide (fifty days after Easter).

The militia was made up of Light Horse (cavalry) and Dragoons or mounted foot soldiers. The Dragoons carried weapons which could be used better on foot but they rode into battle. Beverley provided a table based on the census lists of 1702 which gave the militia for the following counties:

King and Queen and King William—Lt. Horse 189, Dragoons 509; Gloucester—Lt. Horse 121, Dragoons 473; Middlesex—Lt. Horse 56, Dragoons 143.

If the militia was called out, Beverley stated, and "remained in arms three days and upwards, they are entitled to pay for the whole time, but if it prove a false alarm and they have no occasion to continue out so long they can demand nothing."

The muster of the Lower Troop of Middlesex on that September day in 1730 was probably made up of Dragoons since the weapons listed for issue included carbines (muskets were used by mounted infantry in this period).

The exercises may have included target practice, horsemanship and drilling, but warfare with the Indians was waged in the woods and did not follow conventional drills.

One writer described a muster held in 1710 in Henrico County before Governor Spotswood in this manner:

> Dressed in hunting shirts and linsey-woolsey blouses, with knives in their belts and squirrel tails dangling from their caps, they marched in cadence while the supply corps whistled and shouted at pack horses loaded with implements and rations.

A muster served a military purpose, but it provided recreation and social contact as well. Horse racing and visits to the ordinary usually followed the exercises. Conviviality was often the outcome if not the purpose of the muster.

The Discovery of Tobacco

Give Christopher Columbus the credit or the blame. Known as the Discoverer of the New World, he had to give place to others who preceded him to the North American continent. However, he and his men can take sole credit for another discovery: tobacco which they introduced to the Old World.

When in 1492 the *Santa Maria*, flagship of the Admiral of the Ocean Sea, first touched the little island which he named San Salvador, its sailors were astonished to see the native people smoking a rolled up, dry leaf. This was the Europeans' first contact with tobacco, a plant that would become for centuries the basis of the economy in much of the New World.

To the Native Americans, tobacco was a special gift of the Great Spirit. Smoking the peace pipe was used on ceremonial occasions such as the making of treaties between tribes. It was considered an act of friendship with great meaning as the new settlers who participated in the ritual soon realized.

They also used tobacco in religious ceremonies. Virginia author Robert Beverley, writing in 1705 of Indian customs, stated that they offered sacrifice on almost every "new occasion." When they returned from war or a successful hunt they were in the habit of offering tobacco or some part of the spoils in thanks to the Great Spirit. "They burn tobacco instead of incense, to the Sun," he wrote, "to bribe Him to send fair weather or a prosperous voyage."

During the explorations of the islands which Columbus called the "Indies," the visitors learned the habit of smoking the rolled-up dry leaves and carried the custom back to Spain where smoking soon became fashionable. It spread to Portugal and thence to France. In fact the name *nicotine* (Nicot's plant) came from the name of the French ambassador to Lisbon, Jacques Nicot, who sent samples to the French queen as a therapeutic. In

Paris it was soon in wide use. Extravagant claims were made for it as a cure-all; it was used in powder, poultices, salves and cathartics and was referred to as the "fabulous weed."

The habit of smoking spread to England during the reign of Elizabeth I. Sir Francis Drake, Sir Walter Raleigh, and other notables were fond of smoking the clay pipe, a custom borrowed from the Indians. The story that Raleigh's servant doused him with a bucket of water thinking he was on fire when he saw smoke issuing from his mouth is probably only a picturesque legend, but it confirms the fact that the Virginia colonists were already tobacco users when Jamestown was settled.

John Rolfe, best known for his marriage to Pocahontas, is really the father of tobacco culture in Virginia. Finding the native plants here strong and unpleasant, he procured seeds from the West Indies and grew a small crop of the "sweet-scented" variety. His success initiated a craze for growing the plant. The cured leaves could be shipped to England successfully and sold at a profit. In a few years, it became the chief export.

In spite of tobacco's wide-spread use, it had many detractors in the Mother country. Most prominent among them was the Scottish King James I who had succeeded Elizabeth I to the throne. He even published a tract, *Counterblaste to Tobacco*, in which he characterized the use of tobacco as a "custome Lothsome to the eye, hateful to the Nose, harmful to the Braine, and dangerous to the Lungs." Other sober elements in England who had hoped for a profitable trade in timber, ships stores (tar, turpentine and pitch), pig iron and other commodities, were unhappy with the developing tobacco trade, but high profits won out.

Whether Columbus smoked the weed himself is not known. What is known is that of all the gifts of the New World to the Old, tobacco became the most lucrative. Columbus failed to find the Spice Islands, but what he did find brought incredible wealth. Ironically, King James I gave an assessment of the fabulous weed that coincides almost exactly with that of C. Everett Koop, Surgeon General of the United States in the 1990s, some 400 years later.

The Tobacco Trade

The story of the Virginia colony's first century is largely the story of tobacco.

"The leaf shaped the economic, social and political life of those who carried on its culture. It spread the people over the land. It created the plantation pattern," wrote one historian, and "its labor requirements soon meant hordes of African slaves."

The first efforts of the settlers to establish some type of industry had been disastrous. England wanted a colony which would aid its economy, but glass-blowing, started at Jamestown in 1608, failed, iron smelting at Falling Creek on the James was unsuccessful, and shipping timber and naval stores had not produced much money. However, when John Rolfe's first little shipment of tobacco was well-received, the colony had found a product to meet its need.

Three things were favorable for tobacco culture in Tidewater Virginia: the rich soil, temperate climate, and the fact that only unskilled labor was needed.

Cultivation in the beginning followed the simple methods of the Indians. The seeds were planted in hills and covered with the thick mulch of the recently cleared forest land until they sprouted. Suckers were pulled from half-grown plants to produce more vigorous plants; then the mature leaves were pulled and dried in the sun.

In their haste to grow tobacco the settlers did not even dig the stumps from the recently cleared land. A field of tobacco made an untidy appearance, but it grew richly for a few years and produced bountiful crops. When the harvests began to diminish, the planter cleared another field and left the old one to grow up in field pines.

As the trade increased the culture changed somewhat, and by 1627 Virginia was exporting as much as a half million pounds of tobacco annually.

For shipment the colonists used wooden casks of large dimensions called hogsheads. These were made according to specifications issued by the General Assembly. They must be made of seasoned wood, the staves one third inch thick and forty-eight inches long and the top or head of the cask had to be thirty inches in diameter. The dried tobacco leaves were packed so tightly in the cask that the standard weight was 1000 pounds.

Laws were passed to prevent fraud in packing the hogsheads. If a shipper was found guilty of "putting hereinto any stones . . . dirt, sand, stems or other trash" the law read that he was to be penalized 1000 pounds of tobacco.

By the last quarter of the century the industry had grown to the point that it required regulation. Tobacco ports were designated at specific locations where the hogsheads were inspected before loading. By 1691 tobacco ports had been established at the following wharves: Tyndall's Point (Gloucester Point) and West Point on the upper York to serve New Kent County which at that time encompassed also what is now King and Queen and King William Counties. On the Rappahannock River there were two, one at Hob's Hole (Tappahannock) and the other on Nimcock Creek (Urbanna), and in Lancaster County there was one on the Corotoman River. The law specified first that "one or two places and no more" be established on each river. However, because of the rapid growth of the trade, the ports soon increased in number.

The great plantations which grew up along the rivers were the first large producers of tobacco. Each plantation usually had its own sailing vessels capable of making ocean voyages with cargo for sale in England. The schooners took loads of sweet-scented tobacco along with a list of the goods the owner wanted brought back on the return voyage. Furniture, china, silver, fabrics, and wearing apparel were purchased with tobacco.

In the colony it was also the medium of exchange. Contracts were made in terms of tobacco and bills were paid in tobacco. The Vestry Book of Christ Church Parish records all transactions from 1663 to 1767 (the closing date) in terms of tobacco. The minister's annual salary was 16,000 pounds of tobacco. One order was for 1000 pounds to be paid to a member for nursing a sick child; another in 1735 was for 1000 pounds for mending the church belfry.

Getting tobacco hogsheads to the designated ports offered some difficulties. A cask could be rolled short distances by hand or it could be pulled by a team of oxen. Vestiges of some of the rolling roads can still be seen. One such in the town of Urbanna was known as "Prettyman's Rolling Road" which leads down to the wharf between high banks. On one side today stands the tobacco warehouse and opposite it on the other side stands the old customs house. The road itself has been worn down some eight feet by three centuries of traffic.

It was not until after the Revolution that the manufacture of tobacco in this country became important. A few snuff factories existed in the north and plug and twist (chewing) tobacco were gaining favor in the tobacco producing states. On the eve of the Civil War, Richmond and Petersburg were the chief centers of the tobacco manufacture in Virginia.

King and Queen County, 1691-1991

"Don't move to King and Queen County," a new resident is quoted as saying. "It has the biggest mosquitoes, the most bugs, and most unfriendly people anywhere, and you can't get up and down the roads for farm equipment!"

Then with a twinkle in his eye he continued, "I've only been here a few months and I love it. I don't want it to get crowded." No doubt he was enjoying its quiet and peaceful atmosphere.

It is true that the county has maintained its rural characteristics to the present. Today there is not an incorporated town and only one restaurant in its entire length. It does not have a supermarket or major grocery chain, a convenience store, dress shop or gift shop. Neither is there a doctor's, dentist's or opthalmalogist's office. The public library at Walkerton is less than five years old. However, Volunteer Fire Companies have been organized at Newtown, Walkerton, and King and Queen Court House, and there are two Rescue Squads, one at Newtown and one at the Courthouse.

Nevertheless, the county is attracting new residents who are impressed with its low tax base, low crime rate, pure water, unpolluted air, quiet atmosphere and its proximity to Richmond, Williamsburg, and Newport News. Developments are currently proliferating along the Mattaponi.

It is certain that one of its greatest attractions is its people. Possessed of high moral character, friendly, helpful, and hard working, they welcome newcomers and make them feel at home.

The year 1991 marks the Tricentennial of King and Queen County. Cut off from New Kent county, it was named for King William and Queen Mary who had ascended the throne of England the previous year. Originally it had included the area of King William County which became a separate entity in 1702.

The seat of government has always been at its present location; however, the courthouse has been burned twice, first in 1828, and again in 1864 by federal troops. The present main building was erected in 1866 using the old foundation. In 1895 the front wing was added and in 1957 the clerk's office, record room, and judge's chambers completed the complex.

Perhaps the most dramatic event to occur in the history of the county was the burning of the courthouse. A flotilla of Union vessels came up the Mattaponi March 10, 1864, and set fire to all the public buildings and private dwellings. Only one building was left standing. This was done in retaliation for the ambush and death of Colonel Ulric Dahlgren who was leading a raiding party through the county.

King and Queen has been called both the "shoe string" and the "string bean" county because of its extreme length and narrow width. It stretches northeast for a distance of sixty-eight miles and is nowhere as much as ten miles in width. It is bounded by the Mattaponi River on one side and on the other for approximately half its length by the Dragon Run. The soil is fertile except for a stretch in the central part known as the "Barrens" where even the pines are spindly. "Bazzard's Roost," an area impossible to locate (it is always a mile or two up the road or a mile or two back, as the joke goes), is probably a part of the "Barrens."

King and Queen has also been called the most religious county in the state because of the large number of churches. Today there are eighteen Baptist churches, twelve of these are black congregations, and six are white. In addition, there are five United Methodist Churches, one Disciples of Christ, and one Episcopal church, Immanuel, which celebrated its centennial in 1984.

The Baptists established themselves strongly before the Revolution. The oldest, Lower King and Queen Baptist Church, was constituted in 1772 and others soon followed. White churches often had a membership as much as fifty percent black. After the Civil War many black churches were formed usually with the assistance and blessing of the former church.

Following the Revolution and the Disestablishment of the Church of England, many of these churches lost members and eventually ceased to exist. Fortunately two buildings from the Colonial period have survived.

Old Church at Shanghai was the upper Church of Stratton Major Parish. It has recently been partially restored to its Colonial appearance. Phase I involved removal of the slate roof, stabilization of the brick walls, and replacement of stained glass windows (not found in colonial churches) with clear glass. The building is owned by an active United Methodist congregation which carried out the restoration. Phases II and III are planned for later.

Erected in c. 1729 as the Upper Church of Stratton Major Parish. Known today as Old Church it belongs to an United Methodist Church.

The lower church of St. Stephens Parish, known as Old Brick Church in colonial days stands near Cumnor and today is known as Mattaponi. Its Flemish bond brickwork and cruciform shape mark it as formerly a Church of England structure. Abandoned and in a sad state of deterioration, it was acquired about 1830 by a Baptist group which repaired it for use. Both churches are listed on the Virginia Landmarks Register and the National Register of Historic Places.

Colonial settlements followed the rivers. Early plantation owners built homes along the waterways for ease of transportation and shipping. Great estates grew up along the entire length of the Mattaponi River: North Bank, Canterbury, Holly Hill, Ingleside, Bewdley, Locust Grove, Hillsborough, Newington, Pleasant Hill, and Laneville among them. Some have remained in the same family for generations.

In like manner, the rich bottom land along the Dragon attracted settlers and led to a chain of 18th and 19th century homes along it: Poplar Grove, Bird Place, Dulcie Dome, Lewisville, Rock Spring, Marialva, Laurel Bank, Piedmont, and Marlborough.

Three of these Colonial buildings are on the Virginia Landmarks Register and the National Register: Holly Hill, Bewdley, and Hillsborough. In addition a section of the village of Newtown in the upper end of the county has been named an Historic District.

Education always has held high priority in King and Queen County. Private boys' schools flourished even before the Revolution. Among the most notable was Donald Robertson's, attended by James Madison and possibly by George Rogers Clark. Fleetwood, near Bruington, Stevensville Academy, and schools at Centerville (Shacklefords) and Newtown existed before the Civil War.

Among the best known private girls' schools were Locust Cottage, at Stevensville, and Green Mount near St. Stephens Church.

The earliest public high school in this part of the state was established at Stevensville in 1907.

Farming has been the basis of the economy since earliest times, but the number of farms is decreasing today. In the first decades of this century lumbering became an important industry. Schooners loaded with lumber were familiar sights on the Mattaponi and York Rivers. Small lumbering businesses are still numerous and the pulp wood industry is thriving.

Ambush and Arson in King and Queen County

Nine year-old Mattie clutched her rag doll and sobbed. Beside her Mrs. Robert Pollard, her aunt, stood stony-faced, still as a statue, but Aunt Dicey, on her other side, scowling ferociously, muttered under her breath, "Them dam' Yankees ain't goin' leave us nuffin'." The racing flames had already engulfed the kitchen, located about twenty yards from the house, its shingled roof igniting quickly. The house itself was slower to burn. Men were inside with torches lighting first the heavy draperies in the parlor and piling Chippendale chairs with cushioned seats near the flames. The brocaded sofa and the faded carpet were added to the mounting pile. Smoke boiled from the chimney as the fire intensified. Soon heat from the roaring furnace cracked the hand-blown window panes and cold March air rushed in to fan the flames. Everyone had been ordered out of the house, and the women stood, a forlorn group, watching their burning home.

The date was March 10, 1864. During the previous night a string of ships had left Yorktown bearing 2700 Union troops under the command of Brigadier General Isaac Wistar. A cavalry detachment of 1100 men was already moving overland from Gloucester Point led by Brigadier General Judson Kilpatrick. Together they formed a retaliatory force ordered to destroy King and Queen Court House, a rural community consisting of the county courthouse, clerk's office, jail, a tavern, a mill, and several widely separated dwellings. The entire population, at this time, including slaves, could not have been more than fifty people. This overwhelming force bore down upon an unsuspecting community. The transports arrived in the early morning and the troops, without waiting for the cavalry, set about carrying out their orders.

Now, behind the burning Pollard dwelling, old Uncle Joshua watched in stunned disbelief as blue-coated soldiers forced the horses from the stalls. His special responsibility, the animals were as dear to him as if they were his own. Mrs. Pollard's pretty chestnut mare reared and snorted as an unfamiliar figure leaped upon her back. "Marse Robert's saddle horse ain't go' let nobody else ride him, I knows," he whispered, cheered by the thought that one of the soldiers would soon be on his back in the barnyard dirt. These men were experienced horsemen, however, and Blackbeard was soon subdued as were two plow horses and four mules. Joshua's heart sank as he saw the cattle loping for the woods. "If de chases after dem de mought fine Marse Robert," he thought, for only he knew the whereabouts of his master! "Go, Mr. Pollard. Hide somewhere," his wife had urged when the first soldiers entered the yard. "They'll hardly harm women and children, but if you put up any resistance, you'll be shot. Go now, please. We'll be all right," she pled, and he had slipped out the rear door unnoticed by anyone but Joshua.

Through the leafless trees the group in the front yard could see smoke rising from the Martin home, a half-mile away. Then a great burst of smoke and flames behind the house told them that the barn had been set on fire. The barnyard was in chaos—squealing pigs, squawking hens, barking dogs and cursing men—but nothing diverted little Mattie who cried piteously as she clung to Susie, her rag doll, the one possession saved from the fire.

"That's a pretty doll ya got there. I'll just take that for my little girl," a bearded man stopped in passing and pulled it from her arms. Forgetting all lady-like instructions so carefully inculcated by her aunt, Mattie's small foot shot from beneath her long woolen skirt and landed a vicious kick on the soldier's shin. It did no good, Susie disappeared into his haversack, lost to her forever.

"Grandma never forgot the loss of her doll, and she never forgave the Yankee soldier either," said Catherine Beane Hall when she recounted the incident.

Less than a mile away another detachment of soldiers was in the act of firing the public buildings. They pulled leather bound court order books dating from the early 1700s from the shelves of the clerk's office and piled them on the floor. Soon the irreplaceable deeds, wills, and marriage registers, so painstakingly written a century or more ago, were burning merrily. The one occupant of the jail was ordered out and it too was set on fire.

To the left behind the courthouse stood one of the oldest buildings there. Built in the early 18th century, it had served as an ordinary and tavern for well over 100 years. Now the soldiers approached to set it ablaze.

"Everybody out. Clear everybody out," shouted the sergeant. He approached Mrs. Tunstall, the landlady, who stood in the doorway, tight-lipped and defiant.

"Please see that everyone is out of the building, madam. Is there anyone sleeping late upstairs?" he asked in an attempt at humor.

"We have a man ill on the second floor. He can't be moved," she answered.

"Can't be moved, you say! We'll move him; men, go upstairs and bring him down on a pallet, if necessary. We have orders to carry out," he barked.

"What's he sick of ma'am? Pneumonia?"

"Smallpox," answered the lady grimly. "We've lost a-many hereabout with it since Christmas."

"Halt. Leave him be. We'll move on to the mill and burn that," snapped the sergeant.

The men, obviously relieved, moved off quickly to Lumpkin's Mill to pillage for grain first and then to destroy a landmark that had served the community for a hundred years. No more! It too was left to burn itself out.

By day's end the buildings of this peaceful, quiet community had been reduced to smoldering ruins.

"Only one building escaped destruction by the temerity and quick-thinking of Mrs. Tunstall," said Carey Hall, former county clerk and life-long resident of the community.

Why had this community, seemingly unimportant from a military standpoint, been the target of such a massive military attack? The answer lay in an abortive raid on Richmond conceived by General Kilpatrick and Colonel Ulric Dahlgren, twenty-one year-old son of Rear Admiral John A. Dahlgren, U.S.N., and carried forward with the approval of both President Lincoln and Secretary of War Edwin Stanton. Mounted in late February, the attack failed miserably culminating in the death of Colonel Dahlgren.

Among the factors contributing to the fiasco were poor communications, lack of knowledge of the area, bad judgment, missed connections, incredibly bad weather and the physical exhaustion of the troops, some having been in the saddle almost constantly for forty-eight hours. On the other hand, Confederate scouts had soon reported Federal troop movements and preparations for defense of Richmond were begun immediately. Thus the surprise element upon which General Kilpatrick had counted heavily was completely lacking; furthermore, Richmond's defenses were stronger than he had believed. Having failed to enter the city, Kilpatrick withdrew east toward Williamsburg and Dahlgren, after failing to make contact with Kilpatrick, then attempted to rejoin Union forces at Yorktown. He crossed the Mattaponi River at Aylett, moving east through King and Queen County toward Gloucester Point. Almost immediately his movements were reported to the Home Guard which kept a close watch on the troop as it moved forward.

Soon after the outbreak of hostilities, a Home Guard, consisting of men too old to enter Confederate service, had been organized in the county. With regularly commissioned officers under the Reverend R. H. Bagby, D.D., as captain, it became a highly effective body. Among its members was Dr. B. H. Walker, who kept a diary covering the period from

July 5, 1862, to May 18, 1864. His entry for March 2, 1864, gives a first-hand account of the ambush of Dahlgren's forces.

> March 2nd*—Yankees reported crossing Pamunkey at Dabney's Ferry and coming this way. Capt. Bagby ordered his company to meet at Bruington at 5 o'clock. Capt. Magruder's and Capt. Blake's companies, of regular army, with us. Passing up the road over Dickie's Bridge I met a man at the fork, one mile this side of Bruington (Capt. Charles G.), who reported the Yankees at Bruington. We laughed at the report, but in a few minutes heard firing and saw members of the Home Guard fleeing toward us, and Yankees pursuing. The men near Butler's old tavern. The interval was a half-mile or more, but one of our men was struck, though not seriously hurt.
>
> Retiring before the Yankees, most of the Home Guard, with Capt. Magruder's command, took the direct road towards Dickie's Bridge and Stevensville. As we came down it was suggested to send a scout in the direction of the River road. Capt. Harrison of Magruder's company volunteered to move across the fields and count them as they passed down the other road. Passed through B.'s & T. M.'s and Philip Bird's into the Cow Trap woods below Belmont. In about five minutes after we reached our point of observation, the Yankees came along and I counted them,—one hundred and seventy men, mounted. We gave them a shot apiece, which they returned. Presently they stopped and seemed to be feeding in Gaines' old field, but we have since learned that it was at Hocklineck. We moved back from the woods into the road, and passing by Stevensville, we joined Magruder, augmented by some of the King and Queen cavalry under Capt. Fox, and Home Guard, etc. Capt. Bagby had already drawn up his men at the forks of the road above Mantapike. Capt. Fox was requested to take charge of the entire force, and arrangements were made to fight them should they attempt to pass. About 10:30 p.m. the enemy were reported moving. Some of our men at the same moment were moving down towards the fork on the Stevensville road, and came in contact with the enemy just as they reached that point. Col. Ulric Dahlgren, seeing the men in the road, rode up and demanded a surrender, snapping his pistol. The man, or men, immediately fired return shots, and then a fusillade began from the northeast corner of the woody slope upon the head of the Yankee column; the enemy hastily retreated. Then our boys gave a tremendous shout and rushed into the road. I noticed a horse struggling in the agonies of death and a man under him, and in a short time another man lying

in the ditch with his feet up against the fence and tree; this last was Col. Dahlgren. Meantime the Yankees were in considerable commotion,—we on our part expecting another attack,—but as they did not advance, we feared an effort would be made to flank us, and so get by. So Lieuts. Nunn and Acree, Cris. Fleet and I moved out to learn about their intentions. We soon became satisfied they were still in the field. We moved down to where the Mantapike road crosses the River road and raised a barricade, awaiting the enemy the rest of the night. Next morning the whole force surrendered,—it produced a thrill of joy. The field presented a disorderly sight,—horses running loose, arms, saddles, haversacks, canteens, silverware, blankets, etc., scattered in confusion. Most of the arms and many of the horses were appropriated by our soldiers. I got a broken-down horse marked "U.S.," Spencer rifle, saddle, etc. My little boy brought in another horse. During the day many prisoners were brought in.

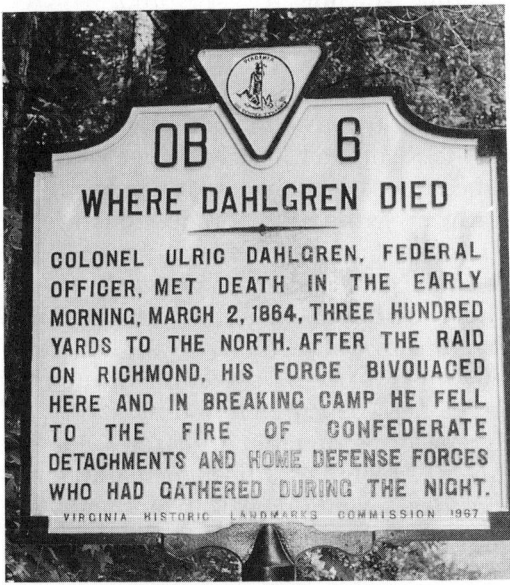

Historic marker on the spot where the Federal Officer, Colonel Ulric Dahlgren, was killed.

Another soldier who happened to be at home on leave recorded his part in the event. Lt. Josiah Ryland, Co. K., Thirty-fourth Virginia Infantry, made the following entry in his diary:

> Wednesday, March 2nd—The writer was at home on furlough, and had the pleasure of taking part in the capture of Dahlgren's raiding party, near Stevensville. Papers found on his person were

said to contain directions to capture and sack Richmond, release all prisoners there, hang Jefferson Davis and his Cabinet, and then make for the Rappahannock River.

The details of the fateful raid were compiled and summarized by Prof. John Pollard, D.D., in a succinct account. Below is his description of the subsequent events of the ambush beginning with the following morning.

> Next morning all surrendered save officers who escaped, but were captured afterwards by Capt. R. H. B. The captures amounted to one hundred and thirty-five soldiers, forty Negroes, beside horses and arms. Major Cook, second in command, left with four or five others during the night, but was taken later.
> Colonel Dahlgren's watch, memorandum-books, and ring were taken; and there was some mutilation (it is said that his finger was cut off in order to remove the ring which he was wearing), which was afterwards regretted. A lock of his hair was preserved by Mrs. Juliet Pollard, and afterwards sent to his father. The morning following, a rude coffin was made, and by and by a grave dug. A few gentle friends were in the act of lowering the body into grave, when orders came to send body to Richmond. This was done and he was buried at Oakwood. Thence it was secretly removed, through Miss Van Lew, a Union sympathizer, to the neighborhood of Laurel, whence again it went north into the hands of his family after the surrender. The admiral wrote to the government immediately after the surrender, enclosing one hundred dollars in gold and asking for the body. As it had been moved from Oakwood by secret Federal sympathizers, the government was greatly perplexed. Evacuation solved the difficulty. Thus the colonel was buried four times.
> Confederate force at Dahlgren Corner on night of March 3, 1864: Cavalry, Pollard, twentyfive men; Captain Fox, fifteen men; Captain Todd, nine men; Captain Magruder, seventy men. Captain Bagby's home guard, thirtyfour men; Captain Halbach (schoolboys), fourteen—onehundred sixtyseven men in all. Only about one hundred of Dahlgren's men were captured, some were killed enroute, and probably some escaped. After the capture large quantities of silverware, rings, and watches, with other valuables, which had been taken from wealthy families, were retaken from the person of the prisoners.

In the abbreviated account above only brief mention is made of Lt. James Pollard of Company H, Ninth Virginia Cavalry,

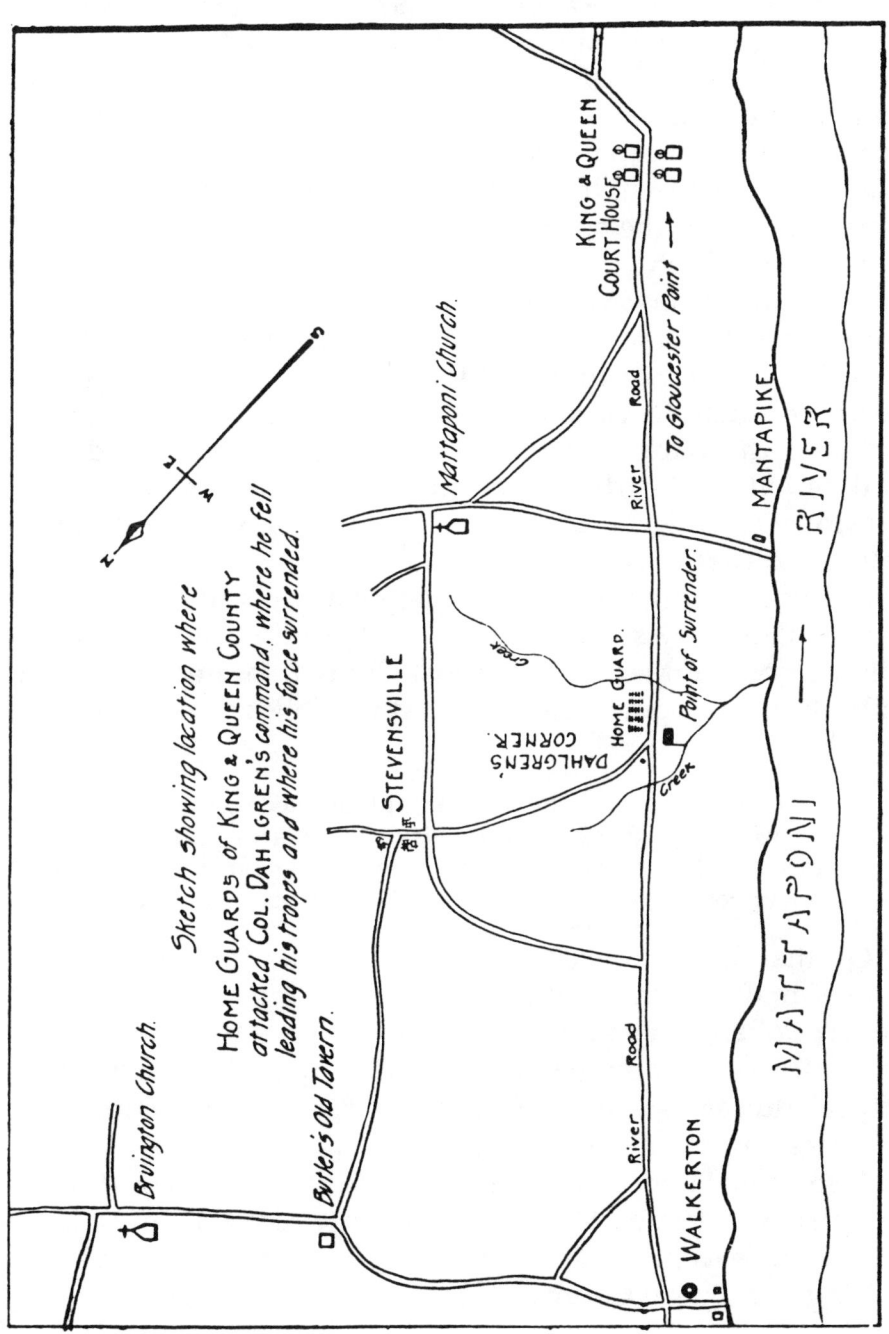

also known as Lee's Rangers. At home on detached leave, Lt. Pollard took initial command of the combined defense forces and set up the ambush on the River Road between Walkerton and King and Queen C. H. This force was augumented by a group of young boys in school at Stevensville and their teacher, Edward H. Halbach. It was one of these boys who, in search of souvenirs, rifled the body of Col. Dahlgren. His finds included a watch which delighted him, some papers and a memorandum book which he turned over to his teacher. These papers, quickly sent to Richmond to President Jefferson Davis, revealed a plot not only to burn the city, but also to put to death President Davis and his entire Cabinet! The Confederacy believed the papers to be genuine; the Union denied their authenticity. The discovery of the papers touched off a controversy between the two governments which was never satisfactorily resolved.

The effects of the raid were felt by many county residents as well as those whose homes were destroyed in retaliation. The Minute book of Mattaponi Baptist Church, located only a few miles from the court house, carried the following entry dated July 9, 1864:

> In consequence of the recent raid of the enemy, and the appropriation by them of the provisions of a large portion of the members of this church, the session of the Rappahannock Association appointed to be held with this church . . . is postponed . . .

On that fateful March day, however, the fires at the court house finally burned out, the Federal troops withdrew, and Robert Pollard returned to take up residence in a wash house which unaccountably had escaped the fire and to carry on his official duties as county clerk. The "smallpox victim" also recovered from his severe headache.

Two years later the first building of the present court house complex was erected to house the county records, now dating, with a few exceptions, from 1864 and to carry on the business of King and Queen County.

*King and Queen County Court House.
Built in 1868 following destruction by Federal troops in 1864.*

Union troops found the Dragon Run a serious obstacle.

Union Troops and the Dragon

The burning of King and Queen Courthouse which took place on March 10, 1864, in retaliation for the ambush and death of Colonel Ulric Dahlgren, U.S. Army, was the subject of a previous article in the *Daily Press*.

The account quoted from the diary of Lt. Josiah Ryland, Company K, 34th Virginia Infantry, from reports of the local Home Guard, and from recollections of local residents who recalled hearing them from their grandparents. All of the information was derived from participants in the event or from Confederate sympathizers.

In recent weeks, I have had the opportunity to read the reports of the Union officers who led the expedition into King and Queen County. Every coin has a reverse side; therefore, it was interesting to compare the accounts of the "other side."

The basic facts are essentially the same: the Union forces destroyed the courthouse, the jail, the mill and dwellings. However, there are details in the Union papers not recorded in the other accounts I have mentioned, and, of course, the point of view is quite different.

Major General Benjamin Butler was in command of the expedition. An excerpt from his initial report, dated March 12, from Fort Monroe, reads:

> While awaiting transportation, I sent a portion of Kilpatrick's cavalry, with a portion of Colonels Onderdonk and Spear's cavalry from my own command up to King and Queen Court House to deal with those citizens, who, claiming to be noncombatants when any force of ours is there, yet turned out and ambushed Dahlgren.

His report continues, describing an attack on the Confederate camp at Carlton's Store in which he states the camp was taken, about 1,200 soldiers and citizens driven out, a number killed and twenty taken prisoner.

The fact that a large camp existed at Carlton's Store, a crossroads settlement about five miles northeast of the court house, is well known. Robert R. Harper, a Civil War historian and relic hunter, spent some weeks in 1985 recovering artifacts from the camp using a metal detector. In an article which appeared in the January 1987 Bulletin of the King and Queen Historical Society, he described the site as he found it and attempted to recreate the camp as it must have appeared when in use.

His account states:

> Huts were dug into the southern slopes and tops of hills in order to obtain the most of the sun's warmth. Log walls six feet high were erected with mud filling the cracks as protection from the cold. Triple rows of huts ran on each side of an old road. Shallow trenches between the tent sites drained into a larger ditch which carried rain water away from the camp.

From the remains of this camp, he recovered a great many artifacts: buttons, buckles, bullets and other items.

It is believed that the camp was laid out in October 1861 as a summer camp to be used by officers defending Gloucester Point, according to Harper. In 1862, it was being used as a rest camp for battle-weary soldiers but by 1864 it had been prepared as a winter camp. Since the attack on the camp occurred in early March, it is possible that some soldiers were still in winter quarters there.

No reference to the attack and capture of prisoners at this camp appeared in the Confederate accounts that I have read.

Topography has always played a significant part in warfare. In the King and Queen expedition, the Union troops found the Dragon Run a formidable obstacle. Brigadier-General Isaac Wistar described it in this manner:

> The Dragon is a swampy, muddy and difficult stream almost all the way to its head. It lies in dense woods with clayey banks and all the bridges have been destroyed. Little or no forage is to be had for some miles from its banks.

In a second dispatch, he continued, stating that heavy rain had raised the river so "that crossing it is impossible, either by fording or bridging. Building a bridge would require half a day at least, besides a long corduroy over the swamp." A corduroy road consisted of six- or eight-inch saplings laid crosswise over the swampy spot. It made crossing possible but exceedingly rough.

The unique features of the Dragon still exist and are now the subject of enthusiastic protection by such organizations as Friends of the Dragon. The only fresh water stream of sufficient flow for industrial purposes, it is, nevertheless, protected because of its scenic beauty, wildlife and its recreational possibilities. At the time of the Union Army's expedition, it served as a protection against further activity in the area.

The attack on the Court House community had been successful from the Union Army's point of view but it had failed to carry out one objective, the capture of the ferryboat at Frazier's Ferry. Brigadier-General Kilpatrick's report to Brigadier-General Isaac Wistar states: The ferry boat "had removed to the other side of the Mattapony and guarded by a company of rebel infantry, who were, of course, inaccessible." Frazier's Ferry crossed from a point a mile or two above the Court House to the King William County shore.

References to the lack of forage for the animals, the horrible roads, heavy rains and the uncooperative attitude of the citizenry by the officers leading the expedition, show that they had no desire to continue the expedition after the main objective had been achieved. Thus the county was saved from further depredations at that time.

Note: I am indebted to Russell Williams of Mascot for the information regarding the Union Army's activity in King and Queen. These papers are excerpts from a compilation of the United States Army reports.

Fort Nonsense

On a high bank overlooking the mouth of Urbanna Creek stands Fort Nonsense, an imposing mansion built c. 1910 by W. W. Marston. "At the time there were evidences of breastworks on the site," wrote Barton Palmer who married Marston's daughter Ruth. "A dwelling on the spot was later moved over to the up creek frontage and the present building constructed for the Marstons."

The origin of this curious name for a dwelling erected in the twentieth century is explained in the following deposition prepared by Palmer a few years before his death. It opens with the usual legal introduction.

> My father, the late Dr. Alfred C. Palmer, was born in Urbanna, Virginia in 1856 on the site adjacent to the north end of the Urbanna Bridge....
>
> At the time of the Civil War he lived in the village. He stated to me that several times the Federal gunboats came up the Rappahannock River and shelled the town not causing much damage....
>
> Some local persons conceived the idea of putting up a camouflaged breastworks on the bluff on the west side of the Creek's entrance. After throwing up some dirt, they took wagon wheels, placing them in position, and mounted tree trunks in between pointing out of the creek, eastward.
>
> On the trip of the gunboats up the river when they came in sight of these "massive" fortifications, they turned around and high-heeled it down the river with nary a shot being fired. From thence this spot has been known as Fort Nonsense.

Palmer, with a keen sense of humor and 81 at the time, wished to leave to posterity a first-hand account of how the name came about.

In a time when most of the able-bodied men were already in the Confederate Army and ordnance and ammunition were scarcer than hen's teeth, the ingenuity and resourcefulness of the town's people are impressive.

How real, however, was the threat that led to the erection of these fortifications?

During the war there was considerable naval activity in the Chesapeake Bay, and some took place in the rivers flowing into the Bay though no major battles were fought there.

By 1863 the Confederate Naval Officer, John Taylor Wood, had made a name for himself as a leader of daring nighttime raids on Federal shipping, and Federal gunboats were constantly on the lookout for him.

In preparation for these attacks, Capt. Wood, with the approval of the Confederate Secretary of the Navy, had constructed several boats capable of carrying fifteen to twenty men with space for ammunition and supplies. In addition, Wood had army wagons fitted with supports and braces so that the boats could be transported overland. This ingenious arrangement made a surprise attack and quick escape possible.

The crews were all volunteers, carefully selected for expertise and courage and their operations were carried out with utmost secrecy.

One of his most successful forays occurred at the mouth of the Rappahannock River in August 1863 when within a three day period, Wood captured two Federal gunboats and three commercial schooners. The capture of the two gunboats, the side-wheeler USS *Satellite* and the 90-ton USS *Reliance* took place in a raging storm off Stingray Point. Rowing their boats from Meachums Creek, the raiders in a surprise attack, boarded the two ships simultaneously and made the capture with only three of Wood's men wounded and no loss of life.

By daylight Wood and his men had the vessels under control and took them up the river to Urbanna where Col. Thomas L. Rosser, commander of the Fifth Virginia Cavalry, was already on hand.

The wounded, both Union and Confederate, were taken to Rosegill where they were treated.

Subsequently the boarding cutters were loaded on the wagons and returned to Richmond.

Such exploits, no doubt, fired the enthusiasm of the Urbanna citizens and led them to erect the fortifications at Fort Nonsense.

Court Days

In the first decades of this century court days rivaled fourth of July and Christmas in importance for many people. Of particular significance were the spring sessions which attracted large crowds.

In Middlesex County, circuit court was held on the fourth Monday in March at Saluda, the county seat on U.S. Rt. 17. If the docket was heavy, it might last for a week. The judge, trial lawyers, possibly jurors, officials, and visitors stayed at Saluda Hotel which occupied the corner diagonally across from the courthouse. Back of it were stables where their horses would be put up for the duration, and the large, three-story brick building provided ample accommodations for the drummers (salesmen), medicine men, and others attending court.

The men of the county came in large numbers, but it was not considered a place for ladies. Vehicles lined the roads for a quarter of a mile in all directions. In the 1920s there were few cars, but buggies, wagons, and road carts were everywhere, according to J. H. (Joe) Major, 92, who attended with his father from the time he was a small boy.

"It was like a carnival," Major said, "There would be music, men playing the French harp, and patent medicine salesmen always putting on a big show. Their medicine would cure anything from corns to backache, they claimed." He laughed at the memory, still vivid and amusing, and continued:

> People would be there selling all kinds of things. Cabbage plants, onion sets, sweet potatoes for bedding. My daddy always got his cabbage plants at March court.
>
> Pollard Woodward and Bob Stubbs [Colonel R. H. Stubbs, member of the Virginia Legislature in the '20s] would get into a

horse race for sure. They'd start up where the high school is now and race down that dirt road to the court house.

Lots of horse-trading went on too. Andrew Dunn, Irving Healy, and Jesse Eubank were great on trading horses.

The thing I remember best though was the food. Early in the morning Dellie Hibble would have a big fire going and a big black iron pot over it. He could cook the best oyster stew you ever ate. He wasn't the only one cooking but his stew was the best, I thought. If I had a dime, I'd get me a bowl of stew and some crackers. On a windy March day it was some kinda good.

There'd be others selling cakes and pies, 'course, sweet potato pie was a big favorite. Then there'd apt to be somebody 'round back peddling whiskey. Had to do it on the sly during Prohibition. That'd lead to a few fist-fights—it all added to the excitement of the day.

While the crowd filled the courtyard, greeting each other, jostling, telling jokes, buying and selling, the business of the court was being conducted upstairs in the courtroom with proper decorum. Judge Clagett Jones followed legal procedure to the letter while dignitaries of the past looked down from portraits lining the walls. Lawyers pled their cases with energy and histrionics and jurors listened with patient attention.

When court recessed for lunch, the judge and other prominent figures crossed the road to Saluda Hotel to enjoy a bountiful meal. Mrs. John H. Pitts, Sr. and later Mrs. Lena Ward Blakey ran the hotel. Both ladies were noted for serving sumptuous meals: fried oysters, ham, baked fowl, vegetables in abundance and a variety of desserts.

April court was the big day in King and Queen County. Judge Jones was sitting judge there also and held court in the courthouse erected after an earlier building was burned by federal troops in 1864.

The same holiday atmosphere prevailed outside. Buggies, wagons, and carts stretched along the dirt roads leading to the courthouse. Back of it were sheds and stables for the horses of those remaining over night. The hotel was located in close proximity. The oldest building in the community, it was spared when federal soldiers burned all the other houses there during the Civil War. Across the road was Garnett Hotel which also accommodated some of the court day crowd. The stables remained into the 1930s, long after automobiles had replaced horses as a means of transportation, according to Carey Hall, former clerk of the court.

Black and white mingled in companionable confusion around the monument erected to the Confederate dead, the clerk's office and the jail, spilling over onto an acre of so of adjoining ground where every type of selling went on.

"The man selling 'Sanitone,' one of those patent medicines said to cure everything from toothache to gout, was my favorite," stated W. S. (Bunny) Beane, a native of King and Queen Court House who said he never missed a court day. He remembered:

> He had two snakes he used to attract a crowd around him. Pete, a Diamond Back Rattler, and Jumbo, the Indian Keel, whatever that is. See, I even remember the names. He'd drape 'em around his shoulders and they'd stay there. Too old to move, I guess. Then he'd stand on a little box and begin to holler:
> "How'd I look? How'd I look?"
> Old Genie Byrd, who didn't like snakes, would holler back, "You looks baaad!"
> Then he'd tell everything the medicine was good for. "Use it internal and external. Makes no difference bound to cure," he'd holler. And you know people would buy it! Those people knew how to fool a crowd. They surely did.

Carey Hall, whose tenure as clerk spanned nearly fifty years, has a fund of fascinating stories about the "great and not so great," that he has known. Hall recounted:

> Col. John R. Saunders, who was Attorney-General of the State for years, always attended court. He had a fantastic memory for names and faces and prided himself on calling his constituents by name. In the 1920s he was a strikingly handsome white-haired gentleman; he'd move through the crowd shaking hands, asking after children, parents, and grandparents.
> "Hello there, Tom," he greeted a middle-aged man clapping him on the shoulder in a friendly fashion.

"How do you do, Colonel," replied Tom, beaming at being remembered.

"Still riding your white horse, aren't you? That's been a good horse, how long you had him?"

"Snowball's near fifteen years old now, but I wouldn't trade him for nothing," answered Tom moving away.

"Colonel, how did you remember that Tom rode a white horse?" asked a bystander in admiration.

"Use your eyes, man. Use your eyes. His blue serge suit was just covered in white hairs," and the Colonel's laugh was loud and long."

Hall obviously loved the story.

King and Queen Court was not unlike other courts. The same display of food, the same buying, selling, and trading went on. Men raced their speed carts from Sandy Point to the Court House, a distance of a half mile, and bragged about their horses. They told tales about their livestock, their crops, and their difficulties. They complained about the weather, the roads, the Republicans, and the preachers; they recalled jokes and pranks that had amused them.

"Gus Waller pulled a good one on Rev. Wright (the much respected black preacher at Union Hope Baptist Church near Ino) once," said Beane.

"Gus killed a hawk a couple of days before court, so he dressed it, cooked it, and served it like baked fowl to the preacher," Bean related. "When someone asked him how he could lie to the preacher, Gus replied, 'I told the truth. I told him it was hen and it was. It was henhawk.' His laughter could have been heard a mile," Beane concluded.

Court days still draw crowds, but they are tame affairs compared with those of the 1920s.

December Sunrise on the Mattaponi River at Hillsborough, mid-18th century home of Mr. and Mrs. W. T. Henley, Sr., Walkerton, Virginia.

Potpourri

To Love a Place

I once thought that a sense of place was a universal characteristic—like the nose on your face, but I know better now. There are thousands of people who have no sense of place. Today's mobile society has produced a rootless generation—people who have moved from place to place so often that they have no feeling of belonging to any particular spot or region.

A few years ago a young man came to me seeking some information on an ancestor, the first of the family to leave England for the New World. He had settled in Middlesex County, Virginia, in the late 1600s and built Wortham Hill. The family had flourished and his progeny had spread westward as had many others, but some had remained. Wonder of wonders for him, a descendant still lived in the house built by the immigrant.

The young man was overjoyed to have found what he was seeking. He became so overwhelmed with the sense of his roots that in his thinking he soon identified completely with the spot where his ancestors had settled.

He told me:

> I have never felt loyalty to any particular place. When I was growing up we moved frequently. My father was with the railroad and was constantly being transferred to another town to leave in a year or two again. When I went to college and was asked where I was from, I honestly didn't know what to say. Now at last I know where I'm from—Middlesex County.

This young man has an acquired sense of place, but numbers of people never experienced what he did. They remain rootless.

My place is rural. I respond to open fields, to growing crops, to new-mown hay, to ripening wheat. To be more specific, I have a strong sentimental tie to the community and region of Tidewater Virginia where I was born. I feel that rootless folk have been denied one of the joys of life whether they realize it or not.

The Northern Neck of Virginia, for instance, is an area which has imbued its citizens with a well-defined sense of place for centuries. Because of its geographical location, bounded by the Rappahannock and Potomac Rivers and the Chesapeake Bay, it became a place set apart. Its residents developed a feeling of belonging to a world that was especially their own. Residents of the Middle Peninsula or the southside of the Rappahannock and the James feel the same, though not perhaps to the same intense degree.

Virginians have been credited with a kind of snobbishness. One quote goes: "To be a Virginian either by birth, marriage, adoption, or even on one's mother's side is an introduction to any state in the union, a passport to any foreign country, and a benediction from above."

Many of us may not be so outspoken, but we agree with this sentiment in principle. Notice the return of the "born-heres." They retire to the old home place or buy a plot of land and build. There is an environmental attraction, a family pull, if you will, that brings them back.

There are three categories of residents in the Northern Neck an informant told me. First, of course, are the "born-heres"; they may trace their ancestry to settlers of the 17th or 18th centuries. Next, are the "brought-heres." They were fortunate enough to marry a native and become permanent residents of the hallowed region. Then there are the "come-heres"—people who visited, found the area beautiful, the climate pleasant, the people charming, and the rural atmosphere just what they wanted. Of course, such groupings can be found, in many other communities. No matter, wherever they are found, the "born-heres" feel a sense of superior status, usually well-hidden on most occasions.

The "born-heres" who return seek out some familiar creek or they buy a few acres near some post office on the verge of closing because the associations of name and place have an attraction, subconscious or conscious.

In my own case, I've not been able to yield to the urge to go back to my birthplace, but the feeling is there, nevertheless. A visit to the house which had been built by my great-grandfather, where my grandfather had reared his children, where my father had spent his boyhood, and which had passed out of the family two generations ago, created in me an almost overwhelming desire to buy it and restore it to its former homelike appearance as a place that still *belonged* although I have no personal memories of it.

What are the things which contribute to this sense of place? What are the memories, often buried in the subconscious, which exert this powerful claim? A friend who had spent many years away from his *place* in Virginia said that the strongest memory which came to him in a wave of nostalgia was that of odors. "Honeysuckle," he said, "and the smell of new-mown hay." These brought on mental pictures that evoked real homesickness.

I think of autumn days as I came home from school seeing the smoke rising from the chimney, smelling the tangy odor of burning oak, hearing the barking of Laddie, my collie dog, as he ran to meet me.

Or mornings when the crowing of the rooster in pre-dawn darkness awakened me; then the lowing of the cows waiting to be milked; the smell of sausage frying in the kitchen and of biscuits smoking hot from the oven.

Or midday when the horses came to the trough to drink, harnesses rattling as they were unhitched from the wagon.

Or evenings, perhaps the most poignant of all, the recollection of the whip-poor-will's mournful cry, seldom heard now. It brings to mind moonlight, the dappled shadows of locust trees stirred by a faint breeze, flickering on the dew-wet grass and that reiterated call; whip-poor-will, whip-poor-will.

This same sense of place brings to my ears, like an echo, speech patterns, long forgotten, but surging from the subconscious to recreate persons and a place.

"That dog ain't worth killing—couldn't trail a fox if it ran in front of him."

"Them cresses will sure make you smack your mouth."

"I'm mighty tired of yo long-winded tales, Josh." I see the crowd in the old store sliding a log of wood into the Wilson heater and leaning comfortably on the worn wooden counter.

A scene at church comes before me: the ladies in Sunday hats and shoes seated on the left with the children; the men in dark suits on the right with the oldest occupying the amen corner and I see the silver goblet of the communion wine passing from hand to hand down the rows in observance of the Lord's Supper. I hear too the stamping of the horses waiting patiently in the churchyard and the voices raised in the closing hymn:

Blest be the tie that binds
Our hearts in Christian love.
The fellowship of kindred minds
Is like to that above.

Virginia is a green state—beautiful at any season. Ride along a country road even in the dead of winter and the bordering pines stand erect and proud, the rich green branches softening the landscape, the tangy pine odor freshening the air and the whispering of the slender needles caressing the ear. Watch for an occasional cedar or holly, not interrupting the greenness, but adding accent to the scene. In spring the greenness has a new intensity with white dogwoods, purple-pink Judas trees, feathery shad bushes and the magenta of blossoming maples providing color to the landscape. Or pass along a swampy area and the odor of laurel (Virginia magnolia) fills the air with over-powering sweetness.

In fall the blending of evergreen and deciduous trees blazing with yellow, red, and brown is a visual feast. Even the old homes surrounded by ancient boxwoods are garlanded in green.

Only those of us who cherish the region, this *place*, will cling stubbornly to such visual memories.

Dwellers along the creeks and rivers have different smells and sounds to create longings. The lap of the waves on the shore, the call of the gull, the creak of the boat tied to the dock, the sight of white-caps on the river or a vee of wild geese flying south bring your place flooding back.

It is the same for mountain folk who love the view of the dark shouldered mountains against a blue sky, the sound of rushing streams or the haven of quiet hollows. We are all cut from the same cloth, we lovers of *place*.

Many writers have given us an opportunity to share their attachment to a special place. Thomas Hardy gave us Wessex; Wordsworth's Lake District comes into perfect focus in "I Wandered Lonely as a Cloud"; Henry David Thoreau penned a prose rhapsody for Walden Pond; Eudora Welty gave us South Carolina and Mark Twain the Mississippi.

A sense of place runs like a golden thread all through our literature, transcending time and place as it takes the reader to places he may never see but which become real through the writer's skill or love.

To love a region is not provincial but universal. It brings out in us the emotions most worth fostering: a sense of identity, a joy based on shared experiences, a tie that keeps us rooted in the soil of loyalty and love. Without this sense of place we cease to be as understanding and appreciative of our past and thus less confident of our future.

If you have no sense of place, you may have many treasured memories, but they are like beads on a string; mine form a rope, strong and enduring.

Feather Beds Were Luxuries

One of our wedding presents when we were married in 1937 was a pair of feather pillows given to us by an elderly friend of my husband's family. The unique feature of this gift was that the lady had saved the feathers and made the pillows herself. She was following a custom common for decades among country people of offering practical gifts to the couple as they set up housekeeping. The modern shower for the bride continues the custom in a different form.

Bedding and bed coverings were luxuries to the early settlers who arrived in this country with tools, weapons, seeds and other necessities but not with mattresses, blankets and sheets. In time great plantations such as Rosegill, Carter's Grove, Rosewell, and Shirley were established and the refinements of living in England were transferred to Virginia. Such estates became almost self-sufficient communities. Smiths made items of iron, craftsmen produced furniture and weavers made cloth for bed-ticking, sheets and materials for clothing using the cotton and flax grown on the plantation. Sheep produced wool which was washed, carded, spun and woven into blankets. Quilt tops were made from scraps, lined, filled with cotton, and quilted, but the feather bed became the ultimate in luxury for comfortable sleeping.

In houses heated only by open fires, bedrooms in winter were always cold. A feather bed provided almost instant warmth to the occupant after the shock of cold sheets wore off. Few things can compare with the soft enfolding warmth of a feather bed. It was wonderful to feel the softness molding itself to the contours of one's body and forming a warm nest in which to cuddle.

The best feathers were secured by live-pluckings. The soft down was taken from the breasts and under the wings of geese and was known as live-down. Eventually, the birds replaced the lost feathers. The process was a little like sheep-shearing because the birds continued to produce.

J. Hoskins Henley, who grew up at Hillsborough near Walkerton in King and Queen County, recalls that every spring Aunt Mary Randolph came to pluck the geese. "White feathers would be flying everywhere," he chuckled. "The geese would swim low in the water for awhile after that until the feathers grew back," he said.

Dan Gill of Remlik Hall Farms in Middlesex says that he sleeps on live-down pillows which came from his grandmother's geese in Chesterfield County.

Feathers were also saved when ducks, geese and other fowl were killed for the table, though they were not of as good quality. Only soft feathers were kept; wing feathers and those with stiff spines were discarded. This practice continued into the 20th century. When I was a child I remember that a half-filled bag of feathers hung on the back porch. When chickens were being dressed my mother would say, "Save the white feathers," and those would be dried and added to the bag for future use.

A feather bed was a large item. To make one meant accumulating feathers over a period of time. When enough were on hand, a cover of hand-woven ticking to fit the bed was made and filled with feathers; then the opening would be sewed tightly to keep the fine feathers from escaping. Even so a few would work their way through the seams as it was used. Finished, the feather bed would be eight or ten inches thick or even more. Bed sizes were not standardized but were built to suit the needs of the owner; some were larger than others, sometimes intended to accommodate several sleepers.

Feather beds became heirlooms. They appeared in inventories in the late 1600s. Major Robert Beverley, a large land owner in Middlesex County, died in 1687. The twenty-four-page inventory of his estate lists three feather beds with bolsters among a variety of other possessions. Such beds appeared in wills to be passed to surviving heirs for they lasted for years. My pillows gave me nearly forty years of continuous service before I discarded them.

I have mixed feelings about the feather beds of my youth. I loved the cozy warmth but making them up was difficult. The covers had to be removed and the bed shaken and beaten to fluff up the feathers. The approved method was to turn the bottom half toward the headboard and shake and beat it and then reverse the process. Sometimes it needed to be shaken from side to side in a similar manner. Altogether it was a strenuous, physical activity, no job for the weak. When it was smooth and even the covers were replaced. To ensure a smooth appearance I used a bed-stick which was long enough to reach from side to side. There was no such thing as "spreading up the bed."

Now the bolster had to be shaken and beaten and the bolster case replaced; the pillows had the same treatment. Finally the pillow shams were carefully spread over the pillows and the process of bed-making was complete.

Spring cleaning required a tremendous upheaval in each room, but the bedroom received the most attention. The bedsteads were taken apart and thoroughly cleaned. Bedbugs were always a possibility and the careful housewife took extreme measures to guard against such a disaster. "An ounce of prevention is worth a pound of cure" is an adage which was taken seriously. An old book, *Housekeeping in Old Virginia* by Marian Tyree (1879), gave recipes for controlling bedbugs, one of which is the following: alcohol—2½ pts., camphor—1 oz., turpentine—1 oz., carbolic acid—½ oz., the mixture was applied with a feather to the cracks and crevices in a wooden bedstead.

The difficulty of controlling bedbugs, nocturnal parasites, which hid in the joinings of the bed frame led to the destruction of many old wooden bedsteads and the popularity of iron on brass beds.

When the beds were reassembled the straw mattress (if there was one) was put on top and the feather bed was placed under it for the summer. The mattresses rested on wooden slats for box springs had not come into use. In the fall the cleaning process was repeated with the feather bed on top of the straw mattress for winter.

This was the period when brides hemmed their sheets and made pillow cases, ornamenting both with fancy needlework: hemstitching, tatting, crocheting or embroidery. Patchwork quilts were made in elaborate patterns, often to be used as coverlets; others were crazy quilts, the pieces assembled according to no particular design. If the bride was able to have a feather bed she felt fortunate indeed.

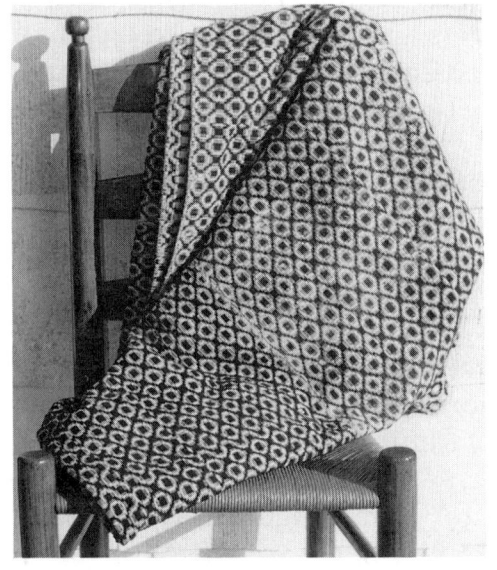

Handwoven blanket. The warp is cotton and the woof is hand-dyed blue wool. Note the seam where the narrow strips from the loom are joined.

One of my prized possessions is a hand-woven coverlet. Made in strips the width of the loom, it is three strips wide and long enough to cover the bolster and hang over the foot and sides of my tester bed. It was among my grandmother's possessions when she was married in 1858.

In heated houses feather beds are not needed as they once were. Most people have discarded them in favor of commercial mattresses which offer better support and are far easier to take care of. I doubt that there is anyone in Tidewater Virginia still sleeping on a feather bed, but some few remain stored for sentimental reasons. They do not rival quilts or woven blankets as heirlooms, but some people remember them from their childhood and smile in reminiscence.

Feathers are still in use for pillows, and down comforters are still the ultimate in luxurious warmth for bed covering. Skiers depend upon down-filled jackets to provide warmth without weight and down-filled sleeping bags are available. L. L. Bean offers a goose-down parka and other woodsmen outfitters provide similar wear, but most use imported feathers. However, the day when housewives saved feathers to provide for household needs is gone. Feathers for commercial use come from large poultry producers.

When Barnhardt Duck Farm, once the largest producer of white Pekin ducks in the U.S., was in operation, sale of duck feathers was a profitable part of the business, according to Elizabeth Barnhardt Sanders. "After the birds had been scalded, the feathers were removed by a mechanical picker, then they were put into a centrifuge where the water was whirled out of them," she explained. "Next they were put into a dryer which transformed the soggy mass into white fluff." Baled, the feathers were shipped to Chicago or New York where down pillows and comforters were made.

"The sale of the feathers often covered the cost of processing the ducks for market," Mrs. Sanders said.

Remlik Hall Turkey Farm did not sell feathers. Turkeys, not being waterfowl, did not produce down. "Occasionally some one would ask for quills from the wings to make a quill pen," said Dan Gill, son of the owner, "but there was no market for turkey feathers."

Feather beds are obsolete today; they have been replaced by mattresses made of many materials: cotton, felt, foam, coils, springs, air, and now the strangely popular water-bed. Mattresses are advertised as offering support for the body, comfort, durability, convenience, even beauty, but not one of these modern solutions to sleeping comfort offers what was the original purpose of the feather bed, softness and warmth. Furthermore, they are not likely to become heirlooms.

Two Virginia Botanists

John Clayton and John Mitchell are two Virginians whose names should be familiar to residents of the Middle Peninsula. Early eighteenth century contemporaries, both men made contributions of enormous value in their time, but few people know much about them today. Furthermore, these men were friends drawn to each other by their absorbing interest in the plant life of Virginia, but there the similarity ends.

A native Virginian, John Mitchell, born in Lancaster County in 1711 of a well-to-do planter family, was sent to England to complete his education. He studied medicine at the University of Edinburgh and returned to Virginia to practice.

In 1734 he purchased property in Urbanna, then becoming a prosperous tobacco port, set up an apothecary shop, a chemical laboratory, and a "physic garden." His primary interest was in growing medicinal plants to be used in the treatment of diseases, but his interest soon widened.

Botany had been a required study in his medical education and he had spent much time in the "King's Garden" at the university observing, classifying, and learning the medical value of the plants there. In Virginia he not only was alert to the familiar herbs, but took a keen interest in the unfamiliar plants which he saw on his long rides visiting the plantations of his patients. He began to collect them for his own garden and to send specimens and seeds to his former teachers in Edinburgh.

Botany was only then becoming a serious study in the great universities of Europe. No system of classification had been devised, but studying specimens, describing and cataloging them occupied many scientists of the day. Dr. Mitchell's packets of seeds and specimens made their contribution to this study.

On the other hand, John Clayton had been born in England in 1693 and had emigrated to Virginia in 1705 with his father who became attorney-general of the colony. Clayton appears to have been well-grounded in Latin, but he was not university-educated. Also he was more than fifteen years older than the young doctor.

Clayton's public career was as a county official. In 1720 he was appointed clerk of the courts of Gloucester County, a position he held for fifty-two years. His duties left him ample time for pursuing his great avocation, the study of plants.

Clayton's interest had a different origin from Mitchell's. As a lad living in Williamsburg, he met the prominent leaders of his time: among them was Mark Catesby, artist and naturalist, who had come to Virginia to study the flora and fauna of the new world. His two-volume *Natural History* contained his paintings of birds, animals and marine life. It is possible that young Clayton, already possessed of a keen interest, became a volunteer assistant.

On his property near the head of the North River in Gloucester, Clayton established a garden to which he transplanted many specimens he found in the wild. He began a correspondence with scientists in Philadelphia and in Europe sending them dried, pressed plants, seeds, cuttings, and roots. Eventually he undertook to catalogue the plants, fruits, and trees native to Virginia, an ambitious undertaking for one working alone.

It was about this time that Dr. Mitchell made his acquaintance. The men lived fifteen or twenty miles apart depending on the route taken. It is probable that Mitchell rode horseback crossing the Piankatank at Turk's Ferry, a designated ferry as early as 1664, to reach Clayton's home. He may, at times, have chosen the longer route using the bridge over Dragon Run, near present-day Saluda. The men delighted in sharing information, exchanging specimens, and discussing plant habitats and uses. Mitchell, no doubt, made contributions to Clayton's catalogue to Gronovius, a Dutch scientist in Holland, who published it without his permission in 1739 under the title *Flora Virginica*. A second volume which appeared in 1743 contained some specimens contributed by Mitchell with due credit given him. Two years later Dr. Mitchell left Urbanna and their association ended.

Flora Virginica was Clayton's greatest achievement, but he was engaged in other activities as well. A recent book by Harriet Frye of Hampton entitled *The Great Forest, John Clayton and Flora* gives a fascinating account of Clayton's life: his association with Robert Beverley, William Byrd and Governor Spotswood, his explorations to the Blue Ridge Mountains, and his famous garden. Her research has contributed new information on the man who was the first colonial botanist, but he was much more.

Clayton's name has been kept alive locally. An historical marker on Rt. 3 in Gloucester proclaims him as a botanist, and garden clubs of both Mathews and Gloucester Counties have been named for him. He has been the subject of two biographies, Frye's being the most recent. His name lives, too, in the botanical name given to a wild flower, Spring Beauty, *Claytonia Virginica*. This honor was bestowed by the Swedish scientist, Carl Linaeus to whom Clayton sent numerous plant specimens.

John Mitchell has not fared so well locally. Because of ill health he returned to England in 1745 and his greatest contributions were made there. He was received by the scientific community of London where he was already known through his extensive correspondence. He was soon invited to join the Royal Philosophical Society. He is credited with making the "most important map in the history of North America." Published in 1755, it showed the extent of the British and French holdings in North America.

A First Edition, Third Impression, of Dr. Mitchell's map was purchased in connection with the Tricentennial of the Town of Urbanna and now hangs in the lobby of the First Virginia-Commonwealth Bank (formerly Bank of Middlesex).

Dr. Mitchell was also honored by the naming of the partridge berry *Mitchella repens* which he discovered in the woodlands of Middlesex. The John Mitchell Garden Club also perpetuates his name.

Mitchell and Clayton, two friends who found the study of plants an absorbing passion, were pioneers in this field of study. They deserve to be better known.

Church Bells

There was a time when the bells from the three churches in Saluda, all in sight of each other, sweetened the air with music on Sunday mornings. First, the mellow tones of the bell of Centenary United Methodist Church announced the hour of worship; next that of Antioch Baptist Church pealed forth; the last, the bell at Clark's Neck (now Saluda Baptist) sent out its call. Never synchronized, the bells rang at different times because services were held at different hours. The still morning air carried the clear notes over the entire village, and even as far as a mile away, saying to all that a welcome awaited at the church of choice. Today when the bells ring, other sounds are apt to drown out the rolling notes.

The steeple and its bell were at one time the identifying mark of a church building. The spire reached heavenward to greater heights for some than others, but the purpose of the structure was clear. Church buildings of the 19th and early 20th centuries followed a familiar architectural pattern. In Middlesex County, for example, there are more than twenty-five church buildings, the majority of which have a steeple of some kind. This feature in a Virginia church is an indication of the period of its construction. Today church architecture is more innovative and exhibits many breaks with tradition.

Few Colonial churches possessed steeples and bells; they also lacked the stained glass windows so popular in the next century. The first house of worship erected in Virginia, the Jamestown church, followed the style of the typical English country church. The tower which remains is the oldest such structure in Virginia.

Why then were bell towers not a common feature of the early Virginia churches? The answer appears to be in the location of the church. In eastern Virginia colonists took up land patents on large acreages so that many miles separated plantations, and villages were rare and far apart. Because church attendance was compulsory and buildings were required by law to be placed within reach of the parishioners, many were in open country. Few of the communicants lived within sound of the bell; moreover, the belfry and bell added to the cost of the edifice.

People who lived clustered together in villages, such as Williamsburg, knew the sound of the church bell. Governor Spotswood presented Bruton Parish Church its first bell in 1711, but rural churches did without.

Christ Church in Lancaster County, built by "King" Carter c. 1732, has no bell; neither is there a bell in the recently restored church of Stratton Major Parish (locally known as Old Church) in King and Queen County nor in the Lower United Methodist Church at Hartfield which before the Revolution was the lower church of Middlesex's Mother Church. Likewise, beautiful Ware and Abingdon Churches in Gloucester County are without bells.

An interesting story exists concerning the bell which once hung in Christ Church (Middlesex). The Parish *Vestry Book* (1663-1767) records the gift of a bell by the Bishop of London in 1718. This gift is explained by the fact that Christopher Robinson, nephew of the bishop, was a vestryman. The *Vestry Book* also recorded that orders were given for "a convenient cupola to be forthwith built at the West end of the Mother Church to hang the said bell in." Evidently the belfry was constructed because in 1734 instructions were given for the church wardens "to be paid 1000 pounds of tobacco for repairing the belfry."

After the Revolution and the subsequent Disestablishment of the Anglican church in 1784, this and many other such churches were abandoned.

Bishop William Meade, author of *Old Churches, Ministers and Families of Virginia* (1857), described the desolation of Christ Church as follows: "Its roof decayed and fell in.... A sycamore tree sprung up within its walls."

Following the Revolution property which had belonged to the Established Church with the exception of the church itself and the graveyard became by law the property of the state. Disposition of such property varied within counties.

In 1814 an Act of the General Assembly of Virginia authorized "the Overseers of the poor in the counties of Middlesex, Mathews and Warwick to recover church plate and bells ... of the said Counties."

Unless the bell had already disappeared, it seems probable that the Bishop's gift was sold and the proceeds used for the needs of the county's poor.

Up to the present what became of the great bell has remained something of a mystery.

However, in recent times a rumor arose that it was hanging in the belfry of Antioch. The idea is intriguing, but the fact is that Antioch's bell bears the inscription of a Philadelphia foundry; it was cast in 1906.

Historically, bells have held an important place in Western culture. In the medieval villages of Europe the dominant building was the church and the dominant feature of the church was the tower with bell and clock. When few people owned a timepiece the village clock served everyone. The bell rang for rising, for midday, and for curfew when the villagers were required to be in their homes. The bell tolled to announce a death, rang merrily for a wedding, clanged frantically as an alarm.

In America, particularly in the New England villages, bells served similar purposes. In rural Virginia a farm bell, usually mounted on a post near the kitchen door, summoned the workmen to meals or to announce an emergency. The cow bell helped the farmer locate a strayed cow. The school bell rang "to open and let out school" and colleges used the bell in the same way. Students at the College of William and Mary as late as the

1930s remember Doc Phillips, the bell ringer, who rang the bell to begin and end classes until automation replaced him. Many remember, too, the clanging of the train bell as it pulled into the station.

The most famous bell in the United States is, of course, the Liberty Bell which rang in 1776 to announce the signing of the Declaration of Independence.

Church bells are heard infrequently today. Less musical sounds flood the airways now and replace the sounds once characteristic of both villages and rural life. Perhaps we are the poorer for it.

This farm bell mounted on a post stands near the kitchen door of Mr. & Mrs. Vernon Norris in Middlesex County, Virginia.

Country Doctors

Once many people owed their lives to the skill and quick thinking of the family doctor. The Hippocratic oath was the code by which he lived.

The doctor's horse and buggy or his model-T Ford was familiar to everyone within the radius of his practice. Office hours were unknown. He treated the few patients who came to his home with perhaps an infected finger, even a broken arm or a deep-seated cough, but his realm was the house call. Usually when the doctor was called the family had already exhausted the home remedies at its command and the patient was in serious need of medical attention. The doctor arrived in the sick room with his medical bag in his hand. His first act might be to thrust a thermometer under the patient's tongue and count his pulse rate. This act would be followed by more careful physical examination. The doctor had none of the present battery of tests, x-rays, CAT scans and other sophisticated devices to aid him in his diagnosis. He had to rely upon his keen observation, his knowledge of circumstances and the situation, and his experience to determine how to treat the patient. Having arrived at a diagnosis, he would open his bag and select the appropriate medication.

The bag was the equivalent of today's pharmacy for rural areas. It was stocked with an assortment of small bottles and phials containing pills and powders with impressive labels. Unlike his predecessor, Dr. John Mitchell, the doctor did not prepare his own medicines by this date. There would be morphine and a few other pain-killing preparations which he used sparingly, doling out a dosage to last only until his return visit. He never left more than a small amount of any medication to be used until he came again and could judge the effectiveness of the dosage.

Pills were counted out into a cup left by the bedside; powders were measured onto a piece of paper which was carefully folded to prevent spilling. There was no charge for the medicine; it was included in the doctor's fee which was modest by today's standards. Sometimes he was paid in produce; he might accept butter, eggs, chickens, a ham or even a load of wood if the illness required many visits.

At an earlier time, the doctor carried a set of apothecary scales along with his medical bag and weighed out the proper dose in grams. Dr. R. H. Woodward's pre-Civil War scales are on display in the Middlesex County Museum as is Dr. Cary Via's medical bag on loan by his granddaughter, Joan B. Curtis of Topping.

If the patient had some extremely serious illness, such as pneumonia, typhoid fever or erysipelas, the doctor might spend the night at the bedside sitting tirelessly through the hours until the fever broke or perhaps the patient died. He was there to comfort the family members as well as to tend sick. Such attention transcended necessity to reach the level of compassionate caring.

Home remedies for minor ailments have always been the province of the women of the household who administered "physick," took care of puncture wounds, cuts, scrapes and bruises in a routine manner. Every home had its store of medicines. No prescription was needed for a dose of Epsom salts, quinine, calomel, or castor oil. The medicine chest usually contained turpentine, camphor, camphorated oil, blue mass pills, and disinfectants such as carbolic acid and peroxide.

Colds usually called for a dose of castor oil. Some parents administered it straight by the tablespoonful; others, more compassionate, poured a little wine into the bottom of the glass, added the oil and topped it with wine. Nothing masked the taste of the stuff which lingered nauseatingly.

A mustard plaster was used for chest colds when a cough persisted. Powdered mustard was mixed with a little flour and water to form a paste which was spread on a square of soft cloth and topped with another cloth. The cold cloth applied to the sufferer's chest sent shivers over his feverish body, but it soon heated up the area loosening the phlegm and resulting in a productive cough. It was an efficacious treatment, but it had to be carefully monitored or the results might be a blistered chest. A variation used by some people was to substitute lard for the water in the mixture. It produced a milder preparation less apt to blister.

Puncture wounds were especially dangerous because they often occurred when children ran barefoot and encountered a nail or a splinter that had been in contact with the soil and so might result in lock jaw. Tetanus bacilli reproduce when shut away from the air so such wounds had to be disinfected and kept open. Tetanus shots were not an option.

Every child was dosed periodically with a purgative. Some families favored Epsom salts; others, calomel, some black draught, an herbal concoction with a horrible taste.

Childbirth was often attended only by a mid-wife. The births which occurred without a doctor in attendance were numerous. Often the doctor was called in only when there were complications.

In every community there was someone resourceful and skilled in the treatment of illness and accidents who could be counted on to come in an emergency. With methods often unorthodox and startling, she effected wonderful cures if old tales are to be credited. Whooping cough and diphtheria were scourges among young children.

"Miss Millie turned him upside down when he was turning blue in the face and shook him and he caught his breath. He'd have died if she hadn't been there!" or "Aunt Sara used cobwebs to stop the bleeding. It worked like magic." and so go the stories of happenings while they waited for the doctor to come.

No doubt it was true that the courage and willingness of these women to take hold and act saved many lives.

Such assistance in no way took away from the high regard which rural families had for the doctor. He knew them more intimately and on a more personal level than anyone else including the minister. He was present at the most critical times, birth, illness, and death. The doctor's very presence lent strength to the family in these times of stress and anxiety.

Medical insurance was non-existent and malpractice suits were unknown. As someone has jokingly said, "The doctor buried his mistakes," but his care was so personal and his devotion to his patients so obvious that no one questioned his good intentions.

The country doctor held an enviable place in the society of his day. Mention the name of Dr. Claybrook Fauntleroy, Dr. Thomas Latane, Dr. Newton DeShazo, Dr. Horace Hoskins, Dr. Virgil Stiff, or a host of others to a person over sixty and the expression softens with nostalgia. Comments such as "He saved mama's life when my little brother was born," "Papa would have lost his leg from blood poison but for him," or "He sat by Aunt Mary all night when she had pneumonia," show the affection in which these doctors were held.

In Middlesex County Dr. Percy Jones, whose practice spanned over forty years, was honored after his death with a memorial shaft erected on the court green. The inscription reads: "A tender, skilled God-fearing physician loved and honored by all. A real friend in need."

Medical care today takes place under very different conditions from those existing at the beginning of this century. But for people who grew up under the visits of the family doctor he remains an almost heroic figure, battling against tremendous odds to bring his skills to his patients at whatever cost to himself. He held a central place in the hearts of each community. He was truly beloved.

Jousting Is Not Dead

Southerners have loved jousting tournaments since before the Civil War. This was the age when a young man's horse was what the sports car is to youth of today. Pitting man and horse in individual competition was thrilling to both riders and onlookers. As the horseman came thundering toward the arches, lance poised and horse in a dead run to spear as many rings as possible, the crowd scarcely breathed, then broke into delighted applause if he succeeded. The colorful trappings, the skill, courage and horsemanship exhibited by the riders appealed to the romantic taste of the period.

Within the last twenty years interest in this medieval sport, once done by armored knights on the jousting fields of England, has shown a sharp increase particularly in Essex County. A jousting tournament is an annual event at Aylett Country Day School at Millers Tavern. In 1981 it was part of the celebrations of the 300th anniversary of the town of Tappahannock and in the summer of 1992 a tournament was part of the observances of the Tricentennial of Essex County. Furthermore, in 1981 a two-day Bicentennial Tournament was held in Yorktown, Virginia, as part of the National Bicentennial Celebration.

All of these events were organized and directed by L. Latane Trice of Walkerton, Virginia.

In reviving the sport, Essex County is following a long-standing tradition as the following from *The Ring Tournament of the United States*, a book devoted to jousting in America, shows:

> At the residence of S. P. Latane, near Miller's Post Office, fifteen young men of Essex County gave a tournament, September 1, 1875. The address was delivered by the editor of *The Tidewater Index*, A. R.

Micou. The winner of the first prize was the well-known horseman, J. W. Dillard, Knight As You Like It. He crowned as queen Josie Jeffries of Tappahannock. J. M. Broaddus, Knight of Little Hope, took second place and crowned as first maid of honor, Ida Motley of Essex. E. M. Sands of V. M. I., Knight of Red, White, and Blue, selected Mattie Williams of King and Queen as second maid of honor. C. B. Newbill of Essex, Knight of Hope, crowned as third maid of honor J. P. Fauntleroy of Essex. Thomas Bagby, a young lawyer of King and Queen, made the coronation speech.

The afternoon program concluded with a ride for a bouquet to be presented to the most graceful horseman. The judges of this event, Susie Haile of Essex, Lucy Latane of King and Queen, and Fannie Scott of Essex, made the award to R. P. Dillard of Essex.

Descendants of several of the persons named in this passage still live in the area. Alex and Peele Dillard of Essex are the great-great nephews of the winner, J. P. Dillard, and relatives of other participants reside in this area as well.

Such events were also common then in Mathews, Middlesex, Gloucester, and the Northern Neck counties.

Basically, jousting requires a rider to spear small rings suspended from an arch with the rider's mount in a dead run. However, details of the sport reveal the high degree of skill, concentration, and horsemanship demanded of the contestants.

First, the field must be approximately two hundred yards long, according to Latane Trice. Three arches set thirty yards apart have a 1½ inch ring suspended from an arm extending over the course. The rings decrease in size as competition continues; sometimes rings as small as one quarter inch in diameter are used before a winner is decided.

The rider needs a distance of at least seventy-five yards to bring his mount to full speed to begin his run and a similar distance to reduce speed to a stop. Timing begins twenty yards from the first arch; the rider must complete the eighty-yard run in eight seconds.

Most lances in current use are seven feet long and made of wood with an eighteen-inch steel tip tapered to a very fine point. Today's lance has a steel fitting midway so that it can be separated for ease in transportation. However, a rider can be original and construct his lance of whatever materials suit his taste and skill.

"Jack Acree of Millers Tavern competed in the Tappahannock tournament of 1981," said Trice, "using a lance made of ¾-inch pipe tipped with a chisel filed to a point and he won."

Mr. Trice possesses a lance used by his father, Harry Trice, made of a single pine shaft tapered to a fine point. It is nine feet long, but today the length has been decreased to the standard seven feet.

As the competition begins, the master of ceremonies calls each knight by the name under which he is riding to take his turn. Leveling his lance as the horse enters the run, the rider rises in the stirrups to give himself a steady arm unaffected by the motion of his steed. Keeping his eye on the ring as he approaches, he attempts to spear all three rings on the point of the lance. Each knight has three rides at the 1½ inch rings; competition continues using smaller and smaller rings until the winner is chosen.

With a large field of riders the competition may go on for hours. Riders usually compete for a monetary prize, a trophy, or simply the honor of winning and placing the crown upon the head of "his fair lady."

Jousting, said to be one of the oldest sports of the Western World, originated in Normandy and spread to England after the Norman Conquest. In Medieval tournaments a knight rode for glory and honor and the privilege of crowning his lady Queen of Love and Beauty. This custom was followed, particularly in the South, for decades.

One social historian (obviously an unromantic Yankee) gives the following rather unsympathetic description of the 19th century tournament. "Costumed in bright silks, the young bloods of the vicinity on their best mounts entered as Knight of the Everglade, Knight of the Black Lance, Knight of the Rappahannock . . . or some other vapid conceit" to compete for the honor of crowning a lady.

From a more sympathetic viewpoint, the events provided color and excitement to rural communities, gave young men an opportunity to display their talents, and gave the young lady crowned a lifelong memory to cherish.

In Middlesex County early in this century, John E. Blakey, Sr., was much in demand to ride tournaments in surrounding counties.

On one occasion he crowned his young daughter Lucy who years later used the same crown to hold her wedding veil when she was married.

In the Jousting Hall of Fame at Mt. Solon, Virginia, are inscribed the names of seven local men who were outstanding horsemen in this demanding sport. They are Jefferson Sinclair of Gloucester, John King of Yorktown, Ashton Yates of Charles City, Joe and Jack Andrews, brothers, of Essex, and Jack Acree and Latane Trice of King and Queen.

The jousting held on August 22, 1992, in Tappahannock attracted riders from Maryland, West Virginia, and other parts of Virginia as well as local participants.

Following tradition, each rider competed under the name of a knight chosen according to his fancy.

The charge of the knights was given by Thomas N. Downing, grandson of the late Congressman Downing.

Master of Ceremonies was L. Latane Trice, veteran of many tournaments, who was awarded a plaque by the National Jousting Association in 1965. It expresses the appreciation of the organization for "26 years of hosting the Tri-State Tournaments."

The revival of this ancient sport in eastern Virginia has been largely due to Trice's efforts and those of a few other devoted horsemen in Essex and King and Queen Counties.

Selected Bibliography

Bagby, Alfred. *King and Queen County, Virginia.* New York: Neale Publishing Co., 1908.

Beverley, Robert. *The History and Present State of Virginia.* Edited by Louis B. Wright, London, 1705, reprint. Chapel Hill: University of North Carolina Press, 1947.

Brydon, George MacLaren. *Virginia's Mother Church and the Political Conditions Under Which It Grew 1727-1824.* Richmond: Whittet and Shepparson, 1952.

Furnas, J. C. *The Americans, a Social History of the United States 1687–1914.* New York: G. P. Putnam's Sons 1969.

Gray, Louise Eubank. *A Patchwork Quilt: Life On A Virginia Farm,* 1910-1920. Lawrenceville, Virginia: Brunswick Publishing, 1989.

Henning, Williams Waller. *The Statutes at Large Being a Collection of All the Laws of Virginia from the First Session of the Legislature in the Year 1619.* Vol. I. Charlottesville: University Press of Virginia. 1819–1823.

History and Progress, Mathews County, Virginia. Reprints from 1949 and 1979 special editions of the Gloucester-Mathews County Gazette Journal. Mathews, Virginia: Mathews County Historical Society, 1982.

Hundley, W. T. *History of Mattaponi Baptist Church, King and Queen County, Virginia.* Richmond: Appeals Press, 1928.

Jones, V. Carrington. *Eight Hours Before Richmond.* New York: Henry Holt, 1957.

Newlon, Howard Jr., Powlett, Nathaniel Mason, *et al. Backsights.* Virginia Department of Highways, 1986.

Robert, Joseph Clarke. *The Story of Tobacco in Richmond.* New York: A. A. Knopf, 1949.

Rountree, Helen C. *Pocahontas's People, The Powhatan Indians of Virginia Through Four Centuries.* Norman: University of Oklahoma Press, 1990.

Shingleton, Royce Gordon. *John Taylor Wood, Sea Ghost of the Confederacy.* University of Georgia Press, 1979.

Vestry Book of Christ Church Parish 1663-1767. Middlesex County, Virginia. Transcribed and indexed by C. C. Chamberlayne, Richmond, 1927.

OTHER SOURCES:

Northern Neck-Middle Peninsula Area Agency on Aging.

Virginia Extension Service.

Interviews with local citizens.